MW00993088

THE WEIGHT LOSS PRAYERS

30 Daily Prayers for Weight Loss Motivation

Kimberly Taylor
TakeBackYourTemple.com

Please see your health care provider for diagnosis and treatment of any medical concerns, and before implementing any nutrition, exercise or other lifestyle changes.

Table of Contents

Introduction

If you are worrying about your weight or your health right now, then I've got a short prayer that can change everything for you.

It's been over 10 years since everything changed in my weight loss struggle. At that time, I was 240 pounds, a size 22, and facing a health crisis. I have a history of high blood pressure in my family. In fact, my grandmother died of a stroke when she was just 47 years-old. I knew in my heart that I was headed in the same direction.

It took my heart speaking to me (literally) to decide to change my health habits for good. I had a severe chest pain that I thought was going to kill me. And while He had my full attention in the midst of that pain, God spoke to me: "It is not supposed to be this way."

At that moment, I had to choose whether to believe Him or not. I chose to believe and that is when my life changed.

That was December 11, 2003. A couple of years after that, God led me to create a website, *www.takebackyourtemple.com*, to inspire others to achieve better health God's way. The title is based on 1 Corinthians 6:19-10, with which you may be familiar:

> "Or do you not know that your body is the temple of the Holy Spirit who is in you, whom

you have from God, and you are not your own? For you were bought at a price; therefore glorify God in your body and in your spirit, which are God's (1 Corinthians 6:19-20)."

God eventually told me the true meaning of the name "Take Back Your Temple." Until that point, I thought of the name as a challenge to people of faith to take back control of their bodies and their health.

But God told me that I was wrong. "Take Back Your Temple" is a prayer.

This prayer asks God to take control of your body and your life so He can use them for His purpose and agenda. You recognize that you are trying to live in your own strength and it just isn't working.

You submit your will to God's will. You recognize that your body is God's temple and you invite Him in to guide you in caring for it. You rely on His strength, not your own.

If you are struggling with your weight right now, then simply ask God to: "Take Back Your Temple."

If you are struggling with destructive habits, simply pray to the Lord in the midst of it: "Take Back Your Temple."

If you are struggling with fear, doubt, depression, stress, worry, or anxiety then invite God into the situation: "Take Back Your Temple."

If you pray that simple, powerful four-word prayer with a sincere heart each time you feel distressed in your health struggle, then it will be answered because it is based upon God's own word.

In faith say, "Thank you Lord. I believe that I receive [say whatever you believe is your level of optimal health] according to Mark 11:24." Actually repeat this until you feel the joy of receiving the gift bubbling up inside of you.

Now, here is the next step. Many people miss this and so do not obtain what they ask for in prayer. Listen as the Holy Spirit speaks to you.

He may remind you how to best eat for your body chemistry; He may teach you ways to manage stress, or He may prompt you to start walking.

Whatever He tells you to do, do it. Walk out His strategy step-by-step, day-by-day. Write it down and review it every day. Don't delay. Each moment you delay is another day in which you are deprived of the very thing for which you prayed.

Prayer was the cornerstone of my success in losing 85 pounds and continues to be the cornerstone of my daily walk with the Lord.

Prayer brings the kingdom of God into your life. Expect three benefits according to Romans 14:17: "for the kingdom of God is not eating and drinking, but righteousness and peace and joy in the Holy Spirit."

Acting in righteousness means that you are empowered to do what God thinks is right. And peace and joy will follow.

My prayer for you is that you put your faith into action every day. According to scripture, you will inherit the promises of God when you put faith and patience to work.

I believe these prayers, devotions, and scriptures will bless you in your weight loss journey. May they strengthen and encourage you every day!

Weight Loss Prayer Day 1: Wisdom

I often receive emails for prayer to help others lose weight. But a couple of years ago, I received a unique request:

> "Could I ask how do I pray an extremely powerful prayer with 100% unwavering faith to ask the "I AM" to have me lose 40 kgs of weight healthy, supernaturally and miraculously?"

I wasn't sure if I understood the request correctly, so I wrote back:

> "It sounds like you are looking for a prayer that will help you lose weight without you having to do or change anything with your eating or exercise. Is that correct?"

> "Yes!" He answered.

Here was my response in part and I hope it helps you too today:

> I applaud you for wanting to achieve a healthy weight. I know how to pray to God for wisdom concerning weight loss, but I do not know a prayer that will enable you to lose weight without you having to do anything. According to scripture, faith without works is dead (see James 2:14-18).

> Even with the great miracles in the bible, action was required. For example, when God parted the Red Sea for the Israelites to cross, he still

instructed Moses to raise his staff. Moses had to do something – act upon his faith.

However, I can give you a prayer so that you can ask God for wisdom on the right daily actions to take to lose weight.

In our Day 1 prayer, I will share the prayer that I wrote for wisdom. However, I'd like to make one important point regarding my response to the gentleman's request; I didn't say that there isn't a supernatural weight loss prayer or that supernatural weight loss isn't possible.

I saw a lady's testimony once on television who said that she lost massive quantities of weight overnight. They showed her before and after pictures. However, I've never known anyone who experienced such a miracle personally nor did that happen with me, so I don't know of a supernatural weight loss prayer.

In my own weight loss success story, God worked my deliverance out step-by-step. God changed my heart supernaturally!

He healed the issues that were causing me to eat excessively. As a result of that and changing in my eating and exercise habits, I lost weight.

During that process, I learned how to trust God and develop a closer walk with Him. Based on that benefit alone, losing weight the old fashioned way was worth it to me.

Today's Prayer:

Gracious heavenly Father, You have said in Your word that if anyone lacks wisdom, all they need to do is ask and You will give them wisdom liberally and without reproach. I come to You in the name of Jesus asking for wisdom to take care of myself so that I may glorify You in my body and my spirit.

Give me the desire to choose foods that bring energy and vitality to my body and clarity to my mind. Give me enthusiasm to exercise so that I may strengthen my body and have the energy to do the things I need to do.

Most of all, Lord, give me wisdom to put You first in my life because You have said that if I seek first your kingdom and all its righteousness, my needs will be taken care of.

Thank you, Father, for giving me the gift of abundant wisdom today. Amen.

Focus Scriptures:

- "If any of you lacks wisdom, let him ask of God, who gives to all liberally and without reproach, and it will be given to him (James 1:5)."

- "Wisdom is the principal thing; Therefore get wisdom. And in all your getting, get understanding (Proverbs 4:7)."

- "The fear of the Lord is the beginning of wisdom, And the knowledge of the Holy One is understanding (Proverbs 9:10)."

Weight Loss Prayer Day 2: Study God's Word

One of my life goals is to learn the bible so well that my cells vibrate with its truth! Okay, it's a lofty goal, but I know that applying God's word is the gateway to a life rich in the fruit of the Spirit – love, joy, peace, patience, kindness, goodness, faithfulness, gentleness, and self control.

In terms of your weight loss goal, it is also essential that you secure your emotions with the truth of God's word. Often emotional instability leads to destructive behaviors, such as emotional eating.

Here are some other benefits that are yours through God's Word, according to Psalm 119. The Word:

- Cleanses your way
- Revives you
- Enables you to receive salvation
- Reminds you of God's mercy
- Teaches you good judgment and knowledge
- Comforts you
- Upholds you
- Reminds you of God's lovingkindness
- Gives you understanding
- Delivers you

If you do not have a time of regular bible study daily, then you are leaving all of these benefits on the table! I recommend in investing in a version of the bible that you understand. For me, the King James Version is hard to understand with the *Thees* and *Thous*. So I use the *New King James Version* or the *New American Standard Version*.

A simple strategy to start a bible reading habit is to visit a site like biblegateway.com and read the *Verse of the Day*. You can always build on that as the Holy Spirit leads you. The benefits you gain from spending time in God's word will be worth far more than the time investment you put into it.

Today's Prayer:

> Lord, I know that Your words are Spirit and they are life. Your Word does not come back to You void but will accomplish that which You please. Father, I ask today for an increased hunger to study Your Word. I treasure Your Word more than my necessary food.
>
> I know that as a follower of Christ, the enemy will try to make me turn from the righteous path. But Your Word is a lamp to my feet and a light to my path. I need Your Word to guide my actions so that I stay on the path that You have set for me.
>
> I can withstand the enemy with the powerful weapons of Spiritual warfare You have given me. So help me to take up the sword of the Spirit today, which is Your holy Word. Help me to study Your Word so that it overflows my heart and issues forth from my mouth. You have promised that I will have what I say according to Your Word.

Speaking Your Word ensures that what I say is in complete agreement to Your will and Your ways. I ask these things in the mighty name of Jesus. Amen.

Focus Scriptures:

- "It is the Spirit who gives life; the flesh profits nothing. The words that I speak to you are spirit, and they are life (John 6:63)."

- "I have not departed from the commandment of His lips; I have treasured the words of His mouth More than my necessary food (Job 23:12)."

- "Your word is a lamp to my feet And a light to my path (Psalm 119:105)."

- "And take the helmet of salvation, and the sword of the Spirit, which is the word of God (Ephesians 6:17);"

- "For assuredly, I say to you, whoever says to this mountain, 'Be removed and be cast into the sea,' and does not doubt in his heart, but believes that those things he says will be done, he will have whatever he says (Mark 11:23)."

Weight Loss Prayer Day 3: Handle Temptations

I re-discovered a powerful weapon to handle temptation recently.

This weapon is so important that Jesus Himself commanded it.

It lines up with one of my favorite sayings from the martial arts: "The best way to win a fight is to avoid getting into one in the first place."

See if you can spot the weapon from Jesus' wise words:

- Jesus prayed: "...And do not lead us into temptation, But deliver us from the evil one (Luke 11:4)"

- Luke 22:40 "...Pray that you may not enter into temptation."

- And to the disciples he said, "...Rise and pray, lest you enter into temptation (Luke 22:46)"

By now, you know the weapon is *prayer*. I pray every day, but must admit I didn't always pray not to enter into temptation.

That was a mistake.

After I saw that Jesus told the disciples to pray not to enter into temptation twice, I remembered 'The Lord's Prayer' in which He also said the same thing.

I had a revelation: It must be **very** important if Jesus said it three times!

How many eating "fights" could you avoid every day if you would only pray not to enter into temptation?

I don't know about you, but I want to avoid all unnecessary fights. Dealing with the necessary fights takes a lot of energy as it is! So I started adding "lead me not into temptation and deliver me from evil" to my daily prayers.

How about you?

Today's Prayer:

> Lord, I pray that I may not enter into temptation. Help me to recognize the enemy's snares so that I can avoid each one.
>
> If I do find myself tempted, then help me to remember that no temptation has overtaken me except such as is common to man, but You are faithful and will not allow me to be tempted more than I am able to bear. You always make a way of escape, so that I can bear it.
>
> Father, I believe in Your Word. Show me the way out of every temptation so clearly that I can't possibly miss it! And then give me the

wisdom and strength to take the path that You have shown me. Amen.

Focus Scriptures:

- "And do not lead us into temptation, But deliver us from the evil one. For Yours is the kingdom and the power and the glory forever. Amen (Matthew 6:13)."

- "No temptation has overtaken you except such as is common to man; but God is faithful, who will not allow you to be tempted beyond what you are able, but with the temptation will also make the way of escape, that you may be able to bear it (1 Corinthians 10:13)."

Weight Loss Prayer Day 4: Emotional Eating

Have you ever heard of the term "gut feeling"? In ancient times, they believed the stomach or waist area was the seat of the emotions, so that is where the expression comes from.

Excessive eating is often an effort to comfort your feelings. When you accept negative thoughts or voices as truth, they shape your choices and ultimately, the direction of your life.

But the bible gives instructions for how to win this Spiritual battle: You must appropriate God's strength and might, taking your thoughts captive to the obedience of Jesus Christ.

In Ephesians 6, it describes the armor of God. The first piece of armor is to gird your waist with truth. Gird means to secure. You must secure your emotions with the truth.

Many people say that "the truth will set you free," but they do not know the definition of truth. The full quote is:

> "Then Jesus said to those Jews who believed Him, "If you abide in My word, you are My disciples indeed. And you shall know the truth, and the truth shall make you free (John 8:31-32)."

Your freedom hinges on the truth that you accept and live by. The only source of truth is God's word. Think about this: When you abide in Jesus' word, it creates your habitation and your habitation shapes your habits!

So ask:

- What do you believe about yourself? Is it what God says about you?

- What do you believe about your ability to overcome? Is it what God says about it?

- What do you believe about your future? Is it what God says about your future?

If not, then you need to find out what God says whenever you are faced with an emotional storm.

God's word is stability, your ultimate source of truth. You will need to renew your mind so that your thoughts are consistent with God's word.

For example if you are angry, then find scriptures related to anger and peace. If you are depressed, find scriptures related to sorrow and joy.

If someone hurt you, you want to read what the scriptures say about forgiveness.

Read those scriptures and meditate on them. You might highlight them in your bible or write them on index cards so that you can find them easily if you need them in the future. In fact, if it is an emotion that you battle a lot, then memorize the key related scriptures.

As you meditate on these scriptures, ask God to show you the truth of the situation, comfort your pain, and minister to your heart. Ask Him also what you should do to handle the emotion.

If you need to cry and are in a place to do it, don't be ashamed. Do it. Allow yourself to feel. You won't fall apart. God will keep you safe.

God gave us emotions for a reason. However, they were meant as a tool for us, not to rule us. They are signals about the beliefs you hold dear. When used properly, your emotions can tell you which beliefs to keep and which to let go of because they do not serve you anymore.

Today's Prayer:

Righteous Father, I admit that I have been struggling with emotional eating for a long time. You said in Your word that Your strength is made perfect in my weakness. I come to you right now to confess this area of weakness to you and ask for Your strength in helping me to overcome it.

I can't do this alone. Help me to experience Your powerful, saving grace today. Fill me with Your love, joy, and peace.

Give me the courage to face the truth about my eating habits and the effects that they are having on my body now and the effects they will have in the future. The truth may hurt, but I'd rather deal with reality of truth rather than the false security of lies. Reveal to me how this habit negatively impacts my spiritual, emotional, and physical health.

Show me the emotions that are driving my behavior and give me the courage to feel them rather than drowning them under food. You have promised to never leave me or forsake me and I trust You will be with me every step of my recovery process.

In the name of Jesus, help me to restore a right relationship with food and put it in its proper place – that of only healing, energizing and nourishing my *body*. Help me to put You first in all things. I thank You Father that You hear me and always hear me. Amen.

Focus Scripture:

- "Concerning this thing I pleaded with the Lord three times that it might depart from me. And He said to me, "My grace is sufficient for you, for My strength is made perfect in weakness." Therefore most gladly I will rather boast in my infirmities, that the power of Christ may rest upon me. Therefore I take pleasure in infirmities, in reproaches, in needs, in persecutions, in distresses, for Christ's sake. For

when I am weak, then I am strong (2
Corinthians 12:8-10)."

Weight Loss Prayer Day 5: Focus

When your weight loss plan doesn't seem to be yielding results as fast as you want, it is easy to become discouraged. If you are in that place, I've got a word to encourage you today.

The other day I heard a pastor talking about Noah's ark. He commented on the fact that God did not instruct Noah to put a series of windows in the sides of the ark, but to only put one window at the top.

You see, God did not want Noah looking at the stormy circumstances outside. Rather He wanted Noah to focus above – to recognize that God was with him and had him covered on every side.

Hebrews 11:3 says: "By faith we understand that the worlds were framed by the word of God, so that the things which are seen were not made of things which are visible."

During challenging times, you need to press into God's word that much harder. If the worlds were framed by the Word of God, then wouldn't it be wise to frame your personal world by the Word of God?

A frame encloses, shapes, and protects. Frames also display the beauty of the picture within to maximum effect.

If your inner world is not framed by the word of God, then all you have is the world's viewpoint as your frame of reference. This will be reflected in your outer world. It will shape your attitude, your language, your actions and your behaviors – all displaying that viewpoint to ugly, maximum effect.

However, when you study God's word, listen to it, meditate on it, and treasure it as much as you treasure physical food, you will start hanging your life on that. You'll begin to build a new frame and because your new inner frame is in harmony with the same frame in which the worlds were built, you will experience more peace, love, and joy in your life.

You will gain new appreciation for the wonderful gift that you received when Jesus Christ became your Savior. Jesus Himself is the Word of God and he made it possible for you to have direct access to God. It was because of His great love for you that He gave His life. The best thing that you can do to express gratitude to a gift giver is to **use** the gift he gives you.

Ask yourself right now – "Is my life framed by God's word or the world and my flesh?"

What do you hang your actions on? What do you hang your decisions on? An easy way to find out is by the gauge of peace. If you have unrest in your spirit about any actions or habits that you are currently engaged in, then something is wrong. Jesus said He left His peace with you and in His peace you should labor to remain!

I say "labor" because the enemy will do everything possible to encourage you to keep your old frame of reference. He knows very well that without God's word, life doesn't work!

However when your life is framed by the word of God, then you will display the grace, beauty and majesty of God Himself – a portrait that unbelievers will desire to own for themselves!

Today's Prayer:

> The bible says that a double-minded man is unstable in all his ways. Lord teach me to be single minded when it comes to pursing those things which edify and glorify You. My highest desire is to honor You in everything that I do, which includes the way I care for my body.
>
> I know that it will be difficult for me to serve You with strength and power if my body is weak and sick. Eating healthy foods and getting regular physical activity help to keep my body strong and powerful, so help me to keep my focus on those things and away from those foods and activities that destroy health.
>
> I desire to frame my world according to Your Word, Lord. I ask this in the name of Jesus. Amen.

Focus Scriptures:

- "Now faith is the substance of things hoped for, the evidence of things not seen. For by it the elders obtained a good testimony. By faith we understand that the worlds were framed by the word of God, so that the things which are seen were not made of things which are visible (Hebrews 11:1-3)."

- "... But let him ask in faith, with no doubting, for he who doubts is like a wave of the sea driven and tossed by the wind. For let not that man suppose that he will receive anything from the Lord; he is a double-minded man, unstable in all his ways (James 1:5-8)."

Weight Loss Prayer Day 6: Mental Clarity

Normally, I am good about listening to the Holy Spirit's direction about what to do, but during a season in my life about 3 years ago, I started ignoring His direction about my eating. In fact, I remember two specific times when He directed me not to eat but I did it anyway.

The first time - I heard that still, small voice distinctly say "Wait 10 minutes" when I wanted to get a second helping. But I got it anyway.

Next, I heard my husband in the kitchen about to get some cereal. I wanted some too, but I wasn't hungry - just tired. I thought I should go on to bed, but instead I ate the cereal.

During the middle of the night, a thunderstorm woke me up. As I lay in bed, I thought about the two instances and asked myself the question: "Why did I disobey the Holy Spirit?" The answer came to me as a shock: It was because I did not want to endure the pain of saying 'No' to myself.

But as I thought about the situation more, I realized I did say 'No' to myself by saying 'No' to the Holy Spirit. He was trying to help me maintain a strong, healthy body and I was rebelling against Him.

It was a sobering reminder that my own sin nature wants to rebel against God. It wanted to cooperate with the enemy's efforts to destroy me, just because giving in to my flesh felt good in the moment. "Oh God, help me!" I prayed silently.

"The little foxes that spoil the vine" came into my mind then. I felt compelled to get out of bed and find the scripture because I knew it was in Song of Solomon. I found it in Song of Solomon 2:15.

> "Catch us the foxes,
> The little foxes that spoil the vines,
> For our vines have tender grapes."

Jesus taught in John 15:8 that we glorify God by bearing much fruit - the fruit of the Spirit is love, joy, peace, patience, kindness, goodness, faithfulness, gentleness and self control.

God wants us to bear fruit by walking in harmony with His Holy Spirit but when we disobey, we allow a fox to nibble at the vine and impair our ability to bear fruit.

Foxes can be a metaphor for the thoughts and actions that you allow to reign in your life that are contrary to God's will for you. Commit to being a fox catcher, watching for those subtle areas of disobedience.

Remember - foxes are crafty creatures, but you can ask God for wisdom and you will be able to outsmart them.

Here is how I handle this now: First, I'm committed to working through all challenges necessary to protect my health. While perfection is not necessary, commitment to the growth process is.

Secondly, here's something I noticed happens when I am tempted to eat when I am not hungry - I feel tension in my head, neck, and sometimes upper chest.

Have you noticed if you have physical symptoms during this time?

Here is what I do then - I intensify the tension by tensing every muscle in my body for 8 seconds - I use 8 because tradition says it's the number of new beginnings.

After that, my body relaxes and I can think more clearly. Mentally, I affirm that my food is to do the will of My Father. So the process is to release the physical tension first, then put myself into a more positive mental state second.

Do that as many times as you need to until your mind is renewed in this area. There are blessings in obedience. God is a rewarder of them that diligently seek Him!

Today's Prayer:

> Father, I know that You are not the author of confusion. You are a God of process and order. Your Word says that You have not given me a Spirit of fear, but of power and love and a sound mind.
>
> I operate with a sound mind today. I will not entertain thoughts of confusion, discouragement and sabotage. Whenever these thoughts try to take over my mind, I push them back through the power of your Word.

I will wait on You because you will help me mount up with wings of eagles. I will run and not be weary. I will walk and not faint. Thank you for giving me the victory today! Amen.

Focus Scriptures:

- "For God is not the author of confusion but of peace, as in all the churches of the saints (1 Corinthians 14:33)."

- "Therefore, having these promises, beloved, let us cleanse ourselves from all filthiness of the flesh and spirit, perfecting holiness in the fear of God (2 Corinthians 7:1)."

- "For God has not given us a spirit of fear, but of power and of love and of a sound mind (2 Timothy 1:7)."

- "But those who wait on the Lord Shall renew their strength; They shall mount up with wings like eagles, They shall run and not be weary, They shall walk and not faint (Isaiah 40:31)."

Weight Loss Prayer Day 7: Discernment

The Holy Spirit gives you power to subdue your old nature and guides you into a life filled with love, joy, peace, patience, kindness, goodness, faithfulness, gentleness, and self-control. However, to receive this wonderful gift, you must be willing to humble yourself, submit to His leading, and obey His direction.

But your old nature fights against this. It is hostile to the things of God. Two attitudes are the hallmark of this old nature:

- "You can't tell me what to do."
- "I want what I want when I want it."

In the Garden of Eden, Eve was tempted to sin because in spite of God taking care of her every need, she did not want to follow Him, but instead wanted to take the reins of control herself (see Genesis 3: 1-6).

The "I want what I want when I want it" attitude lives in the story of Jacob and Esau. Jacob asked Esau to trade his birthright, a double portion blessing that Esau was entitled to as the oldest son, for a mere bowl of stew Jacob had prepared.

Esau was hungry at the time and without barely a thought traded in a double, permanent blessing for a pleasure that would be digested quickly and eliminated from his body (see Genesis 25: 29-34). He came to regret what he did later but by then it was too late.

Don't live a life of regrets over what you might have had and become: Resolve that you will allow the Holy Spirit to empower you to live a life that honors God.

Resolve to be:

- **Courageous:** Being honest with God in prayer about your weaknesses and trusting him to strengthen you to handle them. Also being quick to confess your sins, repent of them (change your heart and mind toward them), put them away, and receive forgiveness.

- **Steadfast:** Recognizing that your old nature never goes away, but you are committed to stay in the fight; you will stand fast in the liberty by which Christ has set you free and you will never entangle yourself again in a yoke of bondage.

- **Humble:** The origin of the "You can't tell me what to do" attitude is Pride. And God resists the proud' but gives grace to the humble. So you must be willing to surrender your will to God and allow Him to direct your life. He will teach you through the guidance of the Holy Spirit as you pray, study His word, and seek His face.

Today's Prayer:

God, your word warns me that the devil constantly roars about, seeking whom he may devour. I ask that you give me discernment so that I can quickly see the snares he has laid to trap me, especially pride, hedonism, and rebellion. Give me the ability to avoid each one.

I will be alert and vigilant as you have instructed. If I happen to fall into affliction, I will cry out to you immediately and I know you will deliver me swiftly. Thank you for your deliverance and your great love for me. Amen.

Focus Scriptures:

- "Be sober, be vigilant; because your adversary the devil walks about like a roaring lion, seeking whom he may devour (1 Peter 5:8)."

- "But He gives more grace. Therefore He says: "God resists the proud, But gives grace to the humble (James 4:6)."

- "You are my hiding place; You shall preserve me from trouble; You shall surround me with songs of deliverance. Selah (Psalm 32:7)"

Weight Loss Prayer Day 8: Self-Discipline

I'm going to introduce you to a word you may or may not have heard before: "Temperance." It's an old-fashioned word that means self-control or moderation.

When you think of a climate that has temperate weather, pleasant images come to mind – clear skies and gentle breezes. There are no extremes of heat or cold. Such an environment is optimal to live in.

Concerning your spirit (lowercase 'spirit' typically means your mind, will, and emotions), you also want your thoughts to be temperate so that your outward habits are temperate. Whenever you do not submit your thoughts, will, and emotions to the obedience of Christ, you leave yourself vulnerable to temptations such as overeating.

Changing the overeating habit starts with a decision. Ask yourself, "Do I control this behavior or does it control me?"

An easy way to tell is to imagine giving up the habit of excess eating from this day forward. Did a feeling of deprivation come over you or are you neutral on it?

If your feelings are neutral or indifferent to it, then you have control over the habit. Consider eliminating it for the sake of others who may be watching you. This is especially true if you appear to be fit and healthy, but eat to excess when you are around friends or family.

They may get the false idea that you overeat all the time when you likely don't.

However, if the vision of giving up the habit makes you feel deprived, uneasy, or fearful, then the habit controls you. You are in danger and need to give up the habit for your own sake. Compulsive overeating can cost you your health or even your life.

So a change of heart and mind is required. This is the attitude you need:

> "I must change this habit. It is no longer acceptable to me. I must change it now. I am committed to changing, no matter how long it takes."

Do you hear the resolve in this statement? It naturally leads to repentance. If you need help with in this area, then take it to the Lord in prayer.

After you've made the decision that you will no longer accept the behavior in yourself, then speak the previous words out loud with as much conviction as you can.

I mentioned that another word for temperance is moderation. Think about a moderator in a debate. Did you know that there is always a debate going on inside of you as to which choices you are going to make each day?

You as the moderator get to choose who wins each debate. Your actions show you which side won! Self-discipline is like a muscle. You have it because it is a fruit of God's Spirit, but you need to use it in order for it to grow.

Today's Prayer:

> I come to you today God asking for the fruit of self-discipline to be cultivated within me. I want to be healthy Spiritually, mentally, and physically.
>
> According to your word, the fruit of the Spirit is love, joy, peace, patience, kindness, goodness, faithfulness, gentleness, and self-control. My desire is to walk in the Spirit so that I will not fulfill the lust of the flesh. Help me to keep my feet on the straight and narrow path always. Amen.

Focus Scriptures:

- "But the fruit of the Spirit is love, joy, peace, longsuffering, kindness, goodness, faithfulness, gentleness, self-control. Against such there is no law. And those who are Christ's have crucified the flesh with its passions and desires (Galatians 5:22-24)."

- "I have been crucified with Christ; it is no longer I who live, but Christ lives in me; and the life which I now live in the flesh I live by faith in the Son of God, who loved me and gave Himself for me (Galatians 2:20)."

- "I say then: Walk in the Spirit, and you shall not fulfill the lust of the flesh (Galatians 5:16)."

Weight Loss Prayer Day 9: Patience

One morning I was jump roping, reflecting, and frankly feeling sorry for myself. God had promised me a wonderful blessing and it hadn't materialized in the timeframe that I expected. I was talking to God about it and telling Him, "I don't feel like I'm any closer to having what you said. In fact, I feel like I am further away from it!"

And immediately, He answered me, "I know what you feel like. What does your faith like?"

The question startled me but I answered back, "My faith like is that I know all things work together for the good of those who love God and are the called according to His purpose. I know that I love God and I am the called according to His purpose. Therefore, all things are working together for my good, including this situation." (Romans 8:28)

Then I also remembered that the word says that the just shall live by faith (Romans 1:17). Nowhere does it say the just shall live by feelings! All believers have been justified by faith in Jesus Christ, therefore we live by faith.

The "feel like" versus "faith like" issue comes up a lot, especially when people make New Year's Resolutions. They start out well, but sooner or later they quit because "I just don't feel like doing this today." And today stretches into tomorrow, next week, and soon the year is gone and they are no closer to becoming the person they want to be than before. In fact, they are further away because they've practiced the old habits for another year, which makes them more entrenched and harder to break.

I don't always feel like taking care of myself. I don't always feel like exercising. I don't always feel like eating healthy. But my faith likes both of those things because in order to maximize my ministry to others, it helps to be physically energetic, healthy and vibrant! So faith controls my actions.

So my question to you is this...are you making health decisions based on "feel like" or "faith like"? If by "feel like" what will be the consequences if you continue to live this way? Write the consequences down in as much detail as you can. Make it vivid and real so that you can really see yourself living with them. Not fun, huh?

Every day, I see or read about people who are destroying their bodies, health, and lives because they are living by feelings and not by faith. It is sad because they are choosing to live less than God's best for them.

Today, resolve to learn what God's word says about health and make this year one in which you act to take care of yourself, not according to feel like, but according to faith like! You will receive wisdom and strength to do this by God's spirit. All it takes is a big decision and a little faith!

Today's Prayer:

> Lord, I ask you to help me not to grow weary in well doing, for you have promised that I will

reap in due season if I do not faint. Please cultivate the fruit of patience within me. I am confident that I will attain the promise of health if I stay on course with practicing good daily health habits.

Help me to recognize when thoughts of discouragement are trying to get me to quit and help to immediately pluck those thoughts out of my mind. I will replace them with encouraging thoughts and recommit to seeing this process through until I reach my goal. As you have been patient with me, so I will be patient in seeing positive changes manifested in my body. In Jesus mighty name I pray, Amen.

Focus Scriptures:

- "And let us not grow weary while doing good, for in due season we shall reap if we do not lose heart (Galatians 6:9)."

- "casting down arguments and every high thing that exalts itself against the knowledge of God, bringing every thought into captivity to the obedience of Christ (2 Corinthians 10:5),"

- "that you do not become sluggish, but imitate those who through faith and patience inherit the promises (Hebrews 6:12)."

Weight Loss Prayer Day 10: Appreciate my Body

A few years ago, I was on a health-related message board and one of the women mentioned that she had watched the Ms. Universe competition the previous night. She was feeling depressed because she had compared herself to the beautiful women in the competition...and found herself wanting. I understood completely.

Don't we all do it? We compare ourselves to a beauty queen or Hollywood actress and then beat ourselves up because we don't look like that. In my case, my comparison standard was Halle Berry.

Then one day, it hit me. Although God has blessed Halle Berry with some good genes, her body didn't happen by accident. She works for it. I only see the results; I don't see the sacrifices and discipline that it took to get there.

Halle Berry has taken what she has and has done the best she can with it. She takes care of herself; I can do the same. Now, I will never have Halle Berry's body. But, I can:

- Love and enjoy my body to its fullest extent.

- Keep Psalm 139:14 close to my heart: "I will praise you, for I am fearfully and wonderfully made; Marvelous are your works, and that my soul knows very well."

- Eat to nourish my body and listen to its signals for when to eat and when to stop.

- Eat food that makes me beautiful inside and out.

- Exercise because it is fun, not view it as a punishment for allowing myself to become overweight.

- Look for fun ways to move throughout the day, doing everything from Latin dancing, to climbing stairs, to jump roping, to skipping, to hula hooping.

You know what? When I made that attitude adjustment and focused on what I have and what I can do instead of wasting energy comparing myself to others, I lost weight and became fit.

Best of all, I added color to a life that was previously drab.

Now, I can't wait to get out of bed to discover what crazy way I'm going to come up with to move my body. It feels so good. I don't do it for a wedding, class reunion or any other external goal. I do it for me.

You can either drag yourself through life or dance through it. I choose to dance. How about you?

Today's Prayer:

I praise You that I am fearfully and wonderful made. Your work is marvelous and that my soul knows very well. Your word says that you rejoice over me with gladness and singing. Thank you for giving me this body as my home to live in while I am on this earth. Because I value Your gift, I do everything I possibly can to learn how to take care of my body and apply what I learn.

I no longer criticize my body. When I insult myself, I realize I am insulting the one whom You have created. My body is what it is today. However, I know that the choices I make today will either make my body stronger tomorrow or worse. Help me Lord to make wise choices in my health habits. Help me to choose foods that give me energy and vitality so that I can give my best to my husband, family, and community. Thank You for clothing me with strength and honor. Amen."

Focus Scriptures:

- "I will praise You, for I am fearfully and wonderfully made; Marvelous are Your works, And that my soul knows very well (Psalm 139:14)."

- "Strength and honor are her clothing;
  She shall rejoice in time to come.
  She opens her mouth with wisdom,

And on her tongue is the law of kindness
(Proverbs 31:25-26)."

Weight Loss Prayer Day 11: Courage

During my weight loss journey, I had to battle discouragement many times. You start a plan with high expectations, but then after a week of hard work, you get on the scale and found that you've "only" lost a pound. Then you are tempted to just give up. After all, your work isn't working!

Here's what I would say to you: "Perhaps things aren't moving as fast as you hoped, but at least you are moving in the right direction!"

That is certainly better than the millions of people who are unhappy with their weight or have a dream in their hearts, but are too scared to do something about it. They are afraid of facing failure.

But I have decided that I'd rather deal with the pain of failure than the pain of regret.

Why? Because at least if I attempt something big and fail, then I have the satisfaction of knowing that I had the courage to **act** on what I believed. Here is a newsflash: Failure is not fatal!

Yes, it stings at the beginning, but failure is a great teacher. You learn what didn't work. Then, you have the choice to keep adjusting your actions until you find what does work or you decide that the goal isn't important enough to you to try again.

On the other hand, regret means that you've condemned your dream to death. Thoughts of "What if..." haunt you. You know that you could become something more, but you just sit on your potential. It's like the man in the parable of the talents in Matthew 25:14-30.

The Lord gave him something to work with, but his ingratitude led him to devalue it and bury it. It was a selfish act; that buried talent couldn't help him, nor anybody else!

If I had to choose what man calls me, I'd rather be branded a failure than a coward.

In the end, the only opinion that matters is God's opinion of you and your opinion of yourself. So don't keep wasting time worrying about man's labels. Focus on getting on with the business of doing what you feel God is calling you to do - knowing He is with you every step of the way.

Today's Prayer:

Lord, I take comfort in knowing that you will never leave me nor forsake me. You told Joshua in Your word to be strong and courageous because You would be with him. I can be strong and courageous on that same basis.

Each and every day Lord, help me to renew my mind to your presence and perfect love for me. Your perfect love will cast out all fear.

When I have needs, I know that I can come boldly to your throne of grace where I will find mercy and grace to help in those times of need. I thank you Lord that you have hedged me from behind and before. Because I am covered on every side, then I can move forward in courage.

Focus Scriptures:

- Have I not commanded you? Be strong and of good courage; do not be afraid, nor be dismayed, for the Lord your God is with you wherever you go (Joshua 1:9)."

- "There is no fear in love; but perfect love casts out fear, because fear involves torment. But he who fears has not been made perfect in love (1 John 4:18)."

- "Let us therefore come boldly to the throne of grace, that we may obtain mercy and find grace to help in time of need (Hebrews 4:16)."

Weight Loss Prayer Day 12: Healthy Routine

Abraham Lincoln once said, "Give me six hours to chop down a tree and I will spend the first four sharpening my ax." As a skilled wood cutter, Lincoln knew that he could save himself hours of effort and time with proper preparation.

This is actually a biblical principle as well. Ecclesiastes 10:10 says:

> If the ax is dull,
> And one does not sharpen the edge,
> Then he must use more strength;
> But wisdom brings success.

When it comes to weight loss, are you making things harder than they have to be? I am thoroughly convinced that 90% of Christian weight loss success is due to preparation. You simply order your life so that your daily routine makes losing weight easy rather than hard. Remember: "The secret to achieving your dreams is found in your daily routine."

I heard a minister say once that the enemy operates in the space between knowledge and action. The enemy's plan is keep you from taking action on doing the right thing. He gets you to take your eyes off your goal.

Two examples of this are keeping unhealthy foods within your daily space. Another is mentally discouraging yourself with false images of pain or deprivation at the thought of getting healthy.

When you make up your mind to get healthy and lose weight, expect to be tested in your resolve. The only way to pass these tests is to be prepared for them.

In my own life, I am always tested in my desire to exercise. One thing I have learned about myself is that if I don't exercise first thing in the morning, I will not do it later. I'll either find something more "important" to do or I'll just say "I don't feel like it."

So instead of fighting with myself, I just make it easy to exercise in the morning. I keep my workout sneakers and jump rope together. If I'm doing an exercise DVD I will put it into the DVD player before I go to bed. I will prepare the workout clothes I'm going to wear and sometimes, I will even wear them to bed if I know I'm going to be pressed for time in the morning.

What things can you start doing today that will make it easier for you to reach your ideal weight? How can you order your life so that it supports a healthier lifestyle?

If you are having a hard time motivating yourself, then think about this question: With your current style of living, what shape will your body be in five years from now? Will you be in better health or worse? Close your eyes right now and really experience what it will feel like to have those results.

If you like the results then keep doing what you are doing. But if not, now is the time to start creating a better future for yourself to enjoy.

Today's Prayer:

Lord, teach me to number my days so that I may gain a heart of wisdom and invest my time wisely. Help me to establish a daily routine that enables me to achieve my dreams. Give me guidance to set up a healthy safety zone around myself so that I can reach my health goals more easily, making life-giving choices.

Reveal to me any obstacles that stand in the way of my goals and provide the solutions on how to overcome them. I also ask You to give me wisdom so that I don't lead myself into temptation. Help me to glorify You in all my ways. Amen.

Focus Scriptures:

- "So teach us to number our days, That we may gain a heart of wisdom (Psalm 90:12)."

- "I call heaven and earth as witnesses today against you, that I have set before you life and death, blessing and cursing; therefore choose life, that both you and your descendants may live (Deuteronomy 30:19);"

Weight Loss Prayer Day 13: Learn from Mistakes

In a 2008 edition of 'O' magazine, Oprah wrote that she had regained weight and was back up to 200 pounds. She stated in the article that she was "mad" at herself and felt "embarrassed" about it. She also mentioned that she had an interview with Tina Turner and Cher and when she compared herself to those women, she felt like "a fat cow."

I felt sad just reading that because I understood those emotions. Back in my dieting days, I would beat myself up terribly for what I saw as my lack of discipline. I would call myself names I wouldn't dare call my worst enemy.

Oprah said that the reason for her weight regain was taking herself off her own priority list. Isn't that what happens to some of us? Everything and everyone gets taken care of…except us.

But that is short-sighted; to give the best of ourselves to others, we can't be running on empty!

If I could have advised Oprah at the time, I'd given her the following advice to get back on track. It may help you too:

1. Accept what happened. It's true that you fell asleep at the wheel, but so what? Praise God that He woke you up! You cannot do anything about the past, but you can do something about your present and future. Each day is a new opportunity to start fresh and to try again. And never call yourself a name that you don't want to answer to.

2. Acknowledge where you went wrong. Retrace your steps and discern your vulnerable points. Remember, whenever you make a decision to get healthy, you will be tested on it over and over again. Count on it and be prepared for it. Two of the most vulnerable times for temptation are when you are tired and when you are alone.

The good news is eating healthy, exercising, and getting adequate rest will increase your physical energy and make you less vulnerable to temptation. But you must stick with your plan at all times. If you allow yourself to become run-down again, those old habits are ready to come calling.

Be especially on guard for temptations when you are alone. Pray, praise, study, call a friend during these times. Many times we indulge in temptations when we are alone, thinking "nobody is going to know". But the bible says that what is done in secret comes to light. Keep that in mind and strive to walk in the light at all times by being honest with yourself about your weaknesses and develop plans to deal with them.

3. Accountability is critical. You need support from someone who can help you stay on track. It is too easy to dismiss your goals when you keep them to yourself. Work with a wellness coach or join a support group that can provide advice and accountability, helping you handle problems as they occur. And start keeping a health journal to monitor your diet and exercise for a while. This will keep you honest about what you are doing.

I know it doesn't feel good to be back in this spot. But God loves you no matter what size you are. Keep the setback in perspective. This is not a tragedy; a tragedy is a child who will go to bed hungry tonight. Praise God that you have more than enough food to sustain you. It is blessing and a privilege.

Praise God that you live in a country that allows you to use your talents and gifts to make a difference in the lives of others and not just live for yourself.

I hope and pray that you will learn from this opportunity and allow God to work it for His good and glory. Now let's get moving!

Today's Prayer:

> Lord, thank you for what you've done for me. You are a great Teacher. Who teaches like you? I thank You for Your patience with me, loving me even when I make mistakes. Help me to learn from my mistakes. I'm tired of going around the same mountains over and over again. I am ready to turn North!
>
> Help me to treasure my growth process every day and be faithful to speak Your Word over my life. I expect Your Word to keep working on me. I am grateful that you open doors no man can close and close doors that no man can open. I am thankful that You create a clear path for me that always leads to the center of Your will. Give me eyes to see the path you've established for me and a heart to obey Your teaching. Amen.

Focus Scriptures:

- "Not that I have already attained, or am already perfected; but I press on, that I may lay hold of that for which Christ Jesus has also laid hold of me. Brethren, I do not count myself to have apprehended; but one thing I do, forgetting those things which are behind and reaching forward to those things which are ahead, I press toward the goal for the prize of the upward call of God in Christ Jesus (Philippians 3:12-14)."

- "You have skirted this mountain long enough; turn northward (Deuteronomy 2:3)"

Weight Loss Prayer Day 14: Positive Support

I once took a class on emergency search and rescue techniques and the one principle they drilled into us was this: The first responsibility the rescuer has is to ensure their own safety. After all, if the rescuer themselves become injured, then they won't be able to help anybody.

Unfortunately, I didn't know this principle during one of my many weight loss attempts. I had gone on a diet and had lost about 30 pounds. At that time, that was all I needed to lose to get down to my ideal weight, so I was looking pretty good. A close family member claimed that she wanted to lose weight, yet conveniently prepared peach cobbler three nights in a row. It was one of my favorite desserts. I was being tested, but I did not know it.

At that time, I failed the test. I reverted back to my old eating habits and it wasn't long before I gained all of the weight back.

How much better would it have been if I had said to myself, "I want to have some of this peach cobbler, but it's more important to me that I set an example for her on the right way to eat." Then, I could have either had a smaller portion one night, but refused it the other two.

But I went under and so did she.

That is why, when you are seeking support in your weight loss journey, you select people to support you who are well established in their health habits. You don't want to select people who are in the same shape as you are - or worse.

Pick someone who is willing to engage in activities with you that don't always revolve around food. For a change, you might suggest going to a park to walk, a museum, or a play.

You need an accountability partner who can cheer you on, to be a 'balloon' in your life, spurring you to go higher, rather than a brick dragging you down.

In addition, strive to help encourage others in the battle. In doing so, you will reap a blessing and become stronger yourself.

Today's Prayer:

> Lord, I am grateful that you have set me on the path to better health so that I can fulfill the purpose to which you have called me. I ask that put people in my circle whom I can support and from whom I can receive support. You said in Your word that a three-fold cord is not quickly broken, so it is wise to join with others striving for the same goals so that we can be stronger together rather than apart.
>
> In Matthew 18:19 Jesus said, "If two of you agree on earth concerning anything that they ask, it will be done for them by My Father in heaven." I come into agreement with my

accountability partners that the answers we seek are on the way. We declare victory today Lord! We are Overcomers by the blood of the Lamb and the word of our testimony.

Father, I trust that You have begun a good work in each of us and will complete it unto the day of Christ Jesus. Help us to stay in perfect peace as we keep our minds stayed on you because we trust in you. Help us to celebrate one another's victories, both large and small. Above all, let give you the glory You richly deserve in all things.

In Jesus' name, Amen.

Focus Scriptures:

- "Though one may be overpowered by another, two can withstand him. And a threefold cord is not quickly broken (Ecclesiastes 4:12)."

- "Again I say to you that if two of you agree on earth concerning anything that they ask, it will be done for them by My Father in heaven (Matthew 18:19)."

- "being confident of this very thing, that He who has begun a good work in you will complete it until the day of Jesus Christ (Philippians 1:6);"

Weight Loss Prayer Day 15: Faith to Change

What if you want to work on your weight, but deep down you don't believe that you can change? You might be discouraged, thinking about the times when you tried to lose weight but didn't achieve the results you wanted. So you've concluded that your past experience must mean that your present and future will be the same. And so you are afraid to try again.

But as a child of God, you already have all the faith you need to change: "For I say, through the grace given to me, to everyone who is among you, not to think of himself more highly than he ought to think, but to think soberly, as God has dealt to each one a measure of faith (Romans 12:3)."

God has given you faith and you demonstrated that faith by believing in your heart and confessing with your mouth that Jesus Christ is Lord in your life. With that must come belief in the word of God. Jesus Himself is the living Word.

You have the ability to see with Spiritual eyes and to go to the throne of grace to receive refreshment, revival, wisdom and courage to do everything that God wants you to do.

God's Word says how change is possible: "And do not be conformed to this world, but be transformed by the renewing of your mind, that you may prove what is that good and acceptable and perfect will of God (Romans 12:2)."

God would not write in his Word that you are to be transformed if it were not possible with the Holy Spirit's help.

So to be transformed your work is to renew your mind to God's word daily. His thoughts and ways are higher than yours. Only by learning to think God's way will you be able to fulfill God's will in your life.

Today's Prayer:

Lord, Your Word says that the renewing of my mind transforms me. Help me to be diligent in meditating upon Your Word every day, knowing that I am growing just as a seed planted into the ground. Because others have gotten healthier through Your Word and Your power, then the same can happen for me!

Even though I face challenges, there is nothing that is too hard for You. You know everything I am going through and You give me grace to deal with it. You are the same God who parted the Red Sea, brought new life to barren wombs, helped people defeat enemies, restored sight to blinded eyes, made the lame walk, and raised people from the dead. I know it is a small thing for You to help me with this weight problem. You are omnipotent God. Your power is greater than any situation I face.

Today, I ask You to help me with any areas of unbelief. If there are any areas of blindness or self deception within me that are preventing me from seeing the deliverance in front of me, then reveal it to me. Lord, restore my hope so that I may move forward. You are faithful and I trust You each and every day as you walk with me through the change process.

Focus Scriptures:

- "And do not be conformed to this world, but be transformed by the renewing of your mind, that you may prove what is that good and acceptable and perfect will of God (Romans 12:2)."

- "See then that you walk circumspectly, not as fools but as wise, redeeming the time, because the days are evil. Therefore do not be unwise, but understand what the will of the Lord is. And do not be drunk with wine, in which is dissipation; but be filled with the Spirit, (Ephesians 5:15-18)"

- "'Ah, Lord God! Behold, You have made the heavens and the earth by Your great power and outstretched arm. There is nothing too hard for You (Jeremiah 32:17)."

Weight Loss Prayer Day 16: Strength

For some reason, God loves to wake me up between 3 and 4 a.m. with a word. It's a good thing that I am a morning person – a hold-over from my nursing days!

Anyway, one morning He gave me a great message. It was based upon Isaiah 41:10:

> Fear not, for I am with you; Be not dismayed, for I am your God. I will strengthen you, Yes, I will help you, I will uphold you with My righteous right hand.'

Who sits at God's right hand? Jesus! That Isaiah scripture is one of my favorites but I never made the Jesus connection before now. Jesus is the right hand that God sent to uphold us – he strengthens us, helps us, and leads us into righteousness – right standing with God and guidance on the right way to live.

Jesus was sent to help us who are weak and unrighteous – slaves to sin while we live in this body.

Jesus came to whoop sin's behind (that image makes me smile) – triumphing over it each and every time while He lived in flesh just like ours, being tempted in every way we are tempted. And when the devil tried to kill Him – fighting Him even to the grave – Jesus defeated sin and death in the grave, emerging triumphant in His glorified body.

That is what you have to look forward to in the future as well – no more having to fight against sin in this "body of death" as Paul calls it. You will be truly free.

But until that time, Jesus sent you the Holy Spirit so that you too can gain the victory over your flesh, just as Jesus did when He lived in His earthly body.

To gain the victory and live in freedom, you must commit to the following:

- Being led by the Spirit (Galatians 5:15-18)
- Abiding in God's word so that you know truth (John 8:31-32)
- Set your mind on things of the Spirit (Romans 8:5-6)

As you do these things, the bible promises that you will reign in life.

What a friend and brother, Savior, we have in Jesus! He strengthens and upholds you no matter what you go through!

Today's Prayer:

> Heavenly Father, I need Your strength on this journey! I want Your Holy Spirit to led me every day because I want to fulfill Your will for my life. Every day, I strive to study Your Word so that I can have Your viewpoint on every situation.
>
> I believe Your Word is the truth. I am weakened when I choose to believe lies. I will no longer live according to the enemy's lies.
>
> I set my mind on the things of the Spirit. Meditating on that which is true, noble, and of good report brings me joy. Joy in You gives me

strength. I rely on that strength every day. The quality of my life comes down to the quality of my day and I want quality days, glorifying You. Amen.

Focus Scriptures:

- "I love you, O LORD, my strength. The LORD is my rock, my fortress and my deliverer; my God is my rock, in whom I take refuge. He is my shield and the horn of my salvation, my stronghold. I call to the LORD, who is worthy of praise, and I am saved from my enemies (Psalm 18: 1-3)."

- "I can do all things through Christ who strengthens me (Philippians 4:13)."

Weight Loss Prayer Day 17: Integrity

Consider this scenario: A man is arrested for armed robbery. He serves his time in prison and is released. He completes his parole, making up his mind that he is never going back to prison. Eventually, he gets a job and starts doing well.

On occasion, he sees his old criminal "friends" on the street. He even committed burglaries with some of them in the past. Would you advise this man to start back hanging out with criminals? I'm sure you'd probably answer, "No - not if he wants to stay out of jail!"

But how often do we make up our minds to lose weight, but still want to keep "hanging out" with the same habits that made us obese to begin with?

Being a person of integrity means being whole and undivided. The bible says that being double-minded causes instability. To become successful with weight loss, it is essential that you be of one mind concerning your goal and do everything possible to order your environment to ensure success.

When I made up my mind that I was going to lose weight no matter what in December 2003, it seemed that everything fell into place. I'm not saying that it was always easy, but I had confidence that I was not going to back to the way I used to be.

As long as I gave myself an "out" and treated my health casually, then my mind became pre-occupied with going back to my old habits. I'd tell myself that it was too hard, that I didn't like vegetables, I didn't like to exercise, blah, blah, blah. Pretty soon, I was headed towards "quitsville."

But once I made my mind up that I wasn't going to quit, then I felt relief. I knew even if I felt like quitting, I wasn't going to. Then, my mind became pre-occupied with finding ways to ensure that I wouldn't quit. It was all a matter of focus.

I started looking for healthy foods and recipes that I enjoyed, activities that were fun, and pleasurable ways to reward myself rather than using food to do so. I created a cycle of joy. Once I committed to enjoying the process, then sticking with it became easier.

Today, make up your mind that you will never turn back on your way to better health. Don't be double-minded. Once you decide that you want to live life in a body that is a blessing to you, then you'll start looking for ways to make your desire real.

Today's Prayer:

> Lord, I want to live in a body that is strong, healthy and vibrant. To enjoy a healthy habitation, I must have healthy habits. Help me to create daily habits that glorify You. I know a house divided against itself cannot stand. Only by focusing on pleasing You can I stand fast in the liberty by which Christ made me free!
>
> In the past, I have been double-minded concerning a healthy lifestyle. But all that does

is make it harder to have the healthy body that I desire. With Your help Lord, I decide right now to be single-minded in this area. Many choices exist in this world so I am determined to find foods and recipes that I like. I can also create an exercise program that suits me, step by step.

Where there is a will, there is a way! Help my will to line up with Your will. Only then can I prosper and be in health as my soul prospers. Amen.

Focus Scriptures:

- "Do not be deceived: "Evil company corrupts good habits (1 Corinthians 15:33)."

- "But Jesus knew their thoughts, and said to them: "Every kingdom divided against itself is brought to desolation, and every city or house divided against itself will not stand (Matthew 12:25)."

Weight Loss Prayer Day 18: Power

Back when I was 240 pounds, one of my favorite binge foods was Pepperidge Farm coconut cake. I would often purchase one, totally intending to eat one slice and be content with that until the next day.

But did that ever happen? No.

Instead, I would eat a piece but then the cake would start calling me: "Kim, come eat me...come eat me." To shut up the voice, I would go eat another piece.

Was the voice satisfied then? No. It compelled me to eat another.

And I ate another. Then another. Finally out of complete abandonment I would get the remaining cake and a knife and a fork. I'd end up eating it all.

And just like the night follows the day, the condemnation would start. The same voice that tempted me in the first place would say, "You knew better than that. Why did you buy that cake? You knew that was going to happen. It's only happened 10 million times before!"

Physically, I'd feel bloated, sick, and nauseous. Full of regret.

But you know what? I don't do that anymore. And here is why...

I had to learn to become Spirit led. That was the source of my power to overcome an addiction that consumed my life for over 20 years.

You see, I learned that the Spirit's voice is gentle, one of confidence and comfort, not condemnation. The Spirit's job is to guide you on the path of God's will for your life – and keep you there until you stand before God and He says, "Well done thy good and faithful servant. Enter into the joy of your Lord!"

The Holy Spirit is your Helper. He has a one track mind - to do the will of God.

In contrast, the enemy is two-faced: He will pretend to be your friend, lead you to yield to your weak flesh, and once you've obeyed him, turn around and condemn you for it. He wants you to remain caught up in that destructive cycle because if you are running on his treadmill, following his dead-end plan, you will never fulfill God's plan for your life!

In Acts 1:8, Jesus promised His disciples: "But you shall receive power when the Holy Spirit has come upon you; and you shall be witnesses to Me in Jerusalem, and in all Judea and Samaria, and to the end of the earth."

So if you have received Jesus as your Savior, you have received power. Jesus Himself received the Spirit: "As soon as Jesus was baptized, he went up out of the water. At that moment heaven was opened, and he saw the Spirit of God descending like a dove and lighting on him" (Matthew 3:16).

Jesus only began His ministry after this happened. That is how He could do the powerful works that He did!

When you are led by the Spirit, you will make right decisions every time. Right decisions are ultimately the key to a successful life. The biggest clue that you are making a right decision is that even though your flesh may not like it, you will feel empowered and secure in your Spirit. You will rejoice in the knowledge that you are following God's path and plan.

However when you feel weak, condemned and discouraged by a decision you made – that is your clue that you are allowing the flesh to control you and not the Spirit.

To learn to walk by the Spirit, start now to ask yourself three questions about every decision you face today, no matter how small it is:

"What should I do Holy Spirit?" The bible assures us that if anyone lacks wisdom, God will give it to her if she asks Him (James 1:5)

Whatever the answer, ask **"Does this decision give me peace?"** A hallmark of the Holy Spirit's guidance is peace and security. If you are still wavering or don't think with certainty: "This is what I should do" then continue to ask in prayer and wait before taking action. I believe if God knows your heart is to obey his will, then he will give you clear guidance.

Another way to tell if your decision is Holy Spirit led or just your flesh, then consider the outcome of both sides of the decision and ask yourself, **"Which**

decision empowers me?" If the decision will leave you feeling disempowered or lacking self control it is not of God since self control is one of the fruits of the Spirit. Let go and ask the Spirit to take control once again.

Resist the urge to condemn yourself for your weaknesses. That is the voice of the enemy, not God:

"There is therefore now no condemnation to those who are in Christ Jesus, who do not walk according to the flesh, but according to the Spirit" (Romans 8:1).

See your weakness as an opportunity for you to learn dependence on the Lord. Just like a baby learning to walk in the natural, it will take time to learn to walk by the Spirit. You may have a few stumbles, but eventually you will walk in faith and confidence.

Get in the habit of being faithful in this regard in the small decisions you make every day. Health-related decisions are excellent training for this since you face many of these decisions every day, from what to eat, how much, and whether to exercise.

Embrace these decisions rather than shrinking from them because if you can learn to follow the Spirit's guidance in small areas, then when you must make a big decision, listening and obeying him will be second nature!

And by the way, I still love Pepperidge Farm coconut cake. However, the Spirit leads me not to buy it unless others are around to share it. He knows my weakness and He gives me wisdom concerning it, which I gladly follow since I know it is for my ultimate good. And for that I rejoice!

Today's Prayer:

Lord, Your Word says that the same power that raised Christ from the dead lives in me because Jesus is my Savior. Remind me to use the power that I have to make healthy decisions that glorify You. You set before me life and death, blessing and cursing. You pleaded with Your people to choose life, therefore I choose life and blessing according to Your will.

Thank you for the empowerment of the Holy Spirit to live a life that pleases You. Help me to have ears to hear the Holy Spirit's direction. Help me to feed my Spirit above my flesh. I recognize that when I am faithful with the small decisions of life, You trust me with much more.

Your strength is made perfect in my weakness. Perfect me in Your love, Lord! I embrace this challenge, knowing that the more I cling to You, the more I reflect Your glorious nature. Amen.

Focus Scriptures:

- "But if the Spirit of Him who raised Jesus from the dead dwells in you, He who raised Christ from the dead will also give life to your mortal bodies through His Spirit who dwells in you (Romans 8:11)."

- "I call heaven and earth as witnesses today against you, that I have set before you life and death, blessing and cursing; therefore choose life, that both you and your descendants may live; that you may love the Lord your God, that you may obey His voice, and that you may cling to Him, for He is your life and the length of your days; and that you may dwell in the land which the Lord swore to your fathers, to Abraham, Isaac, and Jacob, to give them (Deuteronomy 30:19-20)."

- "And He said to me, 'My grace is sufficient for you, for My strength is made perfect in weakness.' Therefore most gladly I will rather boast in my infirmities, that the power of Christ may rest upon me (2 Corinthians 12:9)."

Weight Loss Prayer Day 19: Joy

I heard from a young woman once who told me that someone had spoken some devastating words to her as a child and she believed them. As an adult, she now has a poor self image and is afraid to trust people.

It is sad, but it happens to so many people.

Someone plants a negativity seed in your mind – but then you water it, fertilize it, and build fences around it by agreeing with what they said and by meditating on that word.

Soon, it brings forth a harvest of negative results in your life. It robs you of joy.

As I considered the young woman's situation, I thought about a bible story I read that illustrates an important principle behind this.

In the story from 2 Samuel 18:6-8, King David's servants were in a battle with the supporters of David's son Absalom, the people of Israel. Absalom was trying to take over David's throne and had forced David to go on the run. Here is what the scripture said about the battle:

> "So the people went out into the field of battle against Israel. And the battle was in the woods of Ephraim. The people of Israel were overthrown there before the servants of David, and a great slaughter of twenty thousand took place there that day. For the battle there was

scattered over the face of the whole countryside, and the woods devoured more people that day than the sword devoured."

What caught my attention was the last verse about how the woods devoured more people than the sword devoured. In my bible, it gave a little commentary about how those woods were filled with dense brush, vines, and hidden pits in the ground.

David's men survived the woods of Ephraim because they were familiar with the terrain. But the Israelites weren't, became trapped by them, and died there.

The Spirit revealed to me that more Christians are devoured by the woods of Ephraim than the sword. That is, they fail to take their thoughts captive to the obedience of Jesus Christ, so they end up being defeated by dense woods of fear, depression, anger, and doubting (and the bad decisions that go with it), than by any sword of the enemy or the world.

I've got a challenge for you and it's one that I've taken myself. For the next 30 days, clear out some of those dense woods in your mind by making your heart glad with good words, inside and out. Plant good words in your heart and mind through study of God's word.

You can use good words today by:

- Being thankful for who you are
- Being grateful for what you have
- Saying "thank you" to those people who help or encourage you

- Helping others to lift their burdens, whether through sharing a compliment, encouragement, or wisdom

I declare that as you do so, God will bless you with an abundant harvest of strength, peace, and joy!

Today's Prayer:

Lord, I know that life and death are in the power of the tongue according to Your Word. May I speak life over my health efforts so the process is joyful rather than speaking death over my efforts and making the process harder. I want to do the things necessary to make my body a fit habitation for the Spirit of the living God!

If there is any seed of negativity in my thinking, reveal that to me so that I can root it out through the power of Your Word. Your Words are Spirit and they are life. The more I speak Your Word, the stronger and joyful I feel.

I love Your word, Lord. Meditating on Your character and Your Word brings me joy. Joy in You gives me strength, which I need to finish this race strong. Plus, Jesus said that He left His joy in me and it was His desire that His joy in me be full. Lord, fulfill Your joy in me. Amen.

Focus Scriptures:

- "Anxiety in the heart of man causes depression, But a good word makes it glad (Proverbs 12:25).

- "The king shall have joy in Your strength, O Lord; And in Your salvation how greatly shall he rejoice (Psalm 21:1)!"

- "Then he said to them, "Go your way, eat the fat, drink the sweet, and send portions to those for whom nothing is prepared; for this day is holy to our Lord. Do not sorrow, for the joy of the Lord is your strength (Nehemiah 8:10)."

Weight Loss Prayer Day 20: Dealing with Overwhelm

In meditating on the word "retreat," the Holy Spirit revealed to me that many people, especially women, use food as a form of retreat, a retreat from overwhelm or stress because they have come to associate food with rest, refreshment and renewal.

But this is an inferior way to retreat. And overeating eventually leads to more problems, such as weight gain. But when you resolve the cause, the symptom takes care of itself.

God wants you to enjoy food but He also wants you to use it as it was intended – in moderation and to heal, energize, and nourish your body.

When you need a retreat, He wants you to retreat to Him for rest, refreshment, and renewal!

God showed me that the real danger of excess in anything, whether eating or drinking or practicing addictions, is that they dull the ability of the person to hear His voice.

The Holy Spirit speaks to you all the time, but if you are burdened with worries, doubts, fears, overindulgence or addictions, then you cannot hear Him.

And if you can't hear Him, then you can't be led by Him or apply His wisdom to your life.

That is why so many believers are not living victorious lives. They have static in their lives that is preventing them from receiving the Holy Spirit's broadcast.

Jesus' sacrifice on the cross gave you free access to your Father. You need to build times into your day to retreat to him to pray and to meditate on His Word when life overwhelms you. Doing this will renew, refresh and regenerate you so that you can face the challenges of life.

When your belly is full with the living water of the Spirit, then you will not only be refreshed yourself but you will pour out rivers of living water to others. You will supply refreshment to a world that is thirsty for answers, love and significance.

So today, resolve to retreat in the excellent way and go forth, full of the Holy Spirit into the purpose and plans our Father has for you!

Today's Prayer:

>Lord, there are times when life seems too overwhelming and great to bear. And yet, I know that there is nothing too hard for You. If I feel overwhelmed, then all I need to do is to retreat to You and receive refreshment and help.
>
>You promised that rivers of living water will flow out of the bellies of those who believe in You. I need this water so that I will never thirst again. Fill me up, God. Fill me with You so that I will never turn again to worthless things that can hold no water. Thank you, Lord for being my

fountain whose living waters will never fail.
Amen.

Focus Scriptures:

- "He that believeth on me, as the scripture hath said, out of his belly shall flow rivers of living water (John 7:38)."

- "But when the kindness and the love of God our Savior toward man appeared, not by works of righteousness which we have done, but according to His mercy He saved us, through the washing of regeneration and renewing of the Holy Spirit, whom He poured out on us abundantly through Jesus Christ our Savior, that having been justified by His grace we should become heirs according to the hope of eternal life (Titus 3:4-7)."

- "For My people have committed two evils: They have forsaken Me, the fountain of living waters, And hewn themselves cisterns—broken cisterns that can hold no water (Jeremiah 2:13)."

Weight Loss Prayer Day 21: Handle Stress

Did you know that stress can have a serious impact on your weight loss results? It's true. When you are under chronic stress, your body releases a hormone called Cortisol that ultimately causes you to store more fat.

Here's how it works: Cortisol helps your body mobilize energy in case you need to fight or flee to handle danger. But Cortisol also raises your blood sugar level, which prompts the release of another hormone, called Insulin. One of the side effects of Insulin is that it can cause you to store more fat, in particular around your belly.

So you need to do everything possible to manage your stress so you can minimize these effects.

Here are three things you can do to stress less:

1. **Meditate on the person of Jesus Christ.** I used this technique recently in a slow-moving grocery store line. I could feel myself getting frustrated, but I stopped myself and just thought "Lord, I appreciate this opportunity to stand in this line and use this time to reflect on how good you have been to me."

Then, I started thinking about how grateful I am that Jesus saved me from my sins, how that relationship grants me complete access to God's throne of grace, and how I am being transformed into the image of Christ from glory to glory.

As I focused my attention on Jesus, my problem faded into the background and by the time I got to the cash register, I was smiling and my heart was full of joy. Since I had to endure the time waiting anyway, how much better to spend it thinking about my dear Savior rather than murmuring and complaining to myself!

2. **Make Exercise a Regular Game.** Wow, I can hear the groans right now, but hear me out. Exercise is one of the best ways to relieve stress. But here is the key – you have to make it a game to relieve stress. If you make it a chore, it just adds stress.

When you were a kid, nobody had to make you want to play. You naturally ran, skipped, hopped, rolled, spun, danced and just generally enjoyed living in your body. To relieve stress, get back in touch with that kid. I have a hula hoop and I love to use that to exercise because it is fun and doesn't feel like "exercise".

Can you imagine the looks you would get if you skipped around your neighborhood or spun around in your front yard? Wouldn't it be fun to find out?

3. **Listen to Inspirational music.** Remember how in the bible, David was summoned to play music for Saul when a distressing spirit was upon him? You can use the same tactic to help you stay peaceful during stressful times. Check out Amazon.com, iTunes or other sites for inspirational music that can relieve your stress and renew your Spirit.

Now I admit, many of these tips aren't new and you might be saying "I already know that." But knowing something and doing something are different things.

Nothing changes until you do.

Pick at least one of the tips today and do it. And I guarantee you will stress less!

Today's Prayer:

> God, You know this world can be stressful. To keep up, sometimes I feel as if I must be a driven person. Yet You do not call me to be driven, but to be Spirit led. Lead me Lord. Give me wisdom to discern which activities I should keep in my life and which I need to release. I only want to be engage in activities that fit in with Your will. Remove all distractions from my life.
>
> Help me to manage my time properly to eliminate unnecessary stress. Help me to build moments of stillness into my day so that I can be still and know that You are God.
>
> I will create two circles for myself. Within my circle of influence are those things that I can control; within my circle of concern are those things not within my control. Give me wisdom to handle those things within my control in a Godly way. However, I will release those things that I cannot control to my circle of concern. Those are concerns I release to You in prayer.
>
> Thank you Lord that I can cast my care upon You because You care for me! Amen.

Focus Scriptures:

- "Be still, and know that I am God; I will be exalted among the nations, I will be exalted in the earth (Psalm 46:10)!"

- "For as many as are led by the Spirit of God, these are sons of God (Romans 8:14)."

- "Come to Me, all you who labor and are heavy laden, and I will give you rest. Take My yoke upon you and learn from Me, for I am gentle and lowly in heart, and you will find rest for your souls. For My yoke is easy and My burden is light (Matthew 11:28-30)."

Weight Loss Prayer Day 22: Encourage Myself

You need to become your biggest encourager in your weight loss journey because it might be a while before your outer body reflects the positive changes you are making, particularly if you have more than 100 pounds to lose. You want to enjoy the process all along, not just give yourself permission to feel happy only when you have reached your ideal size.

One of the most important lessons I've learned about the importance of encouraging yourself is one I learned in the first year of my weight loss journey. I used to take the train to work every morning and one of the stops just happened to be the building that I work in. However, there was a steep escalator to get from the train station to the building. This escalator has to be at least 40 feet high.

A ritual exists for boarding this escalator. The people who are riding up the escalator stand to the right; the people who are walking up the escalator do so on the left. At first, I stood with the riders on the right. And then something strange happened. I started longing to join the people walking on the left.

I don't know how it happened, but one day I found myself on the left. Walking up that escalator was tough. I only made it about 2/3 of the way up before I saw an opening on the right. I practically jumped into the spot to let the walkers behind me continue on up. My heart felt like it was going to pop out of my chest and sweat made my face shiny.

But I felt good.

It was enough to make me want to do it again.

I did. First I walked up the escalator two days a week and rode three for a few weeks. When that became easier, I added another walking day. So it went until I was able to walk up every day. I never joined the riders on the right again.

As I struggled those months to be able to walk up the escalator, I noticed one thing; if I allowed myself to look up to the top of the escalator, I would see how far it was and I would tell myself that I couldn't make it. The goal seemed impossible. However, if I focused on just making it to the next step, then that seemed doable; I reached the top every time.

That's what praising God and encouraging yourself does. It gives you the strength you need to keep moving on up.

Today's Prayer:

> Lord, You are worthy to be praised! When I lift You up, I am lifted up. So Lord, help me to remind myself of the mighty God I serve. Help me to magnify You whenever I am tempted to magnify my challenges. The bigger you become in my mind, the smaller my challenges look in comparison.
>
> I realize that my weight loss will take happen by process. I am willing to go through the process and give the process the time it needs to

complete. In the meantime, I will devote my attention to fulfilling my purpose in You, not to complaining about how "long" the process is taking.

Help me to be diligent in keeping myself encouraged, Father. Help me to take note of other signs that I am moving in the right direction regarding my health - signs like boosted energy, increased confidence, and greater mental focus. I will praise You for every sign of progress I make! Amen.

Focus Scriptures:

- "And let us not grow weary while doing good, for in due season we shall reap if we do not lose heart (Galatians 6:9)."

- "Not that I have already attained, or am already perfected; but I press on, that I may lay hold of that for which Christ Jesus has also laid hold of me. Brethren, I do not count myself to have apprehended; but one thing I do, forgetting those things which are behind and reaching forward to those things which are ahead, I press toward the goal for the prize of the upward call of God in Christ Jesus (Philippians 3:12-14)."

Weight Loss Prayer Day 23: Enjoy the Process

Are you cursing your efforts to gain good health? It was a question that came to mind as I watched a reality show called 'Bulging Brides' a few years ago.

The show was about women who wanted to get into shape for their weddings. The show gave them a nutritionist and personal trainer to work with them for six weeks to help them accomplish their goals.

I watched two episodes and then could not watch anymore. Neither of the women appeared to be grateful for the help they were getting. They complained to the nutritionist about the healthy food they were asked to eat. They complained to the trainer about the workouts they were asked to do.

It puzzled me because they had taken the time to be on the show, said that they wanted to get in shape, and yet were complaining about doing the very things that would get them what they said they wanted!

They were cursing their efforts because with every complaint, they made following through on their goals that much harder.

And because they despised the effort to gain good health, good health was probably going to be taken away from them. As soon as the wedding was over, they would probably go back to the same habits that made them unhealthy in the first place. It's a self-fulfilling prophecy.

This same principle is mirrored in the bible – consider the Israelites trip to the Promised Land. A trip that should have taken weeks ended up taking 40 years – all because of their complaining, ungrateful attitude, and lack of faith.

What is your attitude about getting healthy? If you are cursing your efforts currently, then it is time to reverse the curse. Start blessing your efforts. Believe me, you will get faster results and those results will last.

You can do this in two ways:

1. Start encouraging yourself. A takebackyourtemple.com reader named Carmen wrote me because she is believing God for healing a thyroid condition, but said it seems like she is not doing anything at all. I smiled because in that same email, this is what Carmen said she is doing:

- Eating high fiber
- Lots of vegetables
- Hardly any sugars
- No processed foods or white flour
- Exercise daily for 60 minutes
- Speaking the Word over her thyroid

You can clearly see that Carmen is doing a lot! So who is telling her that she isn't doing anything? The discouragement is nothing but a trick of the enemy to get her to quit. After all, he knows that getting her to stop pursing health is the 100% way to stop her healing and rob God of the glory from it.

Don't take action based on what you feel. Do it based on what you **know**. God's word says that He wants you to prosper and be in health as your soul prospers. As you take action based on this truth in God's Word, you can be confident that you are bringing His blessings into your world.

2. SMILE when you exercise and eat healthy. Do this even if you don't feel like it at first. Your feelings will soon match your face. It's a miracle! You know that your body language often mirrors your feelings (try feeling depressed without slumping your shoulders and looking downcast and sad – you can't). But it works in reverse too.

I do this neat trick on myself. Whenever I exercise, I plant a big smile on my face showing teeth and everything. Even though my feelings don't always match at first, as I move my feelings start to change. Soon I am moving with more vigor and actually having fun.

With my wide smile, I train my brain to associate pleasure with exercise and it makes me want to work out harder and keep on doing it. It also makes the activity easier and I believe that it helps to burn fat faster and more efficiently with the improved oxygen exchange.

You also bless others if you are smiling while exercising in public. Don't you feel better when you see someone else with a friendly smile? Plus, here is a benefit you may not have considered:
if someone sees you having a good time while

exercising, it might inspire them to start exercising themselves. You both can win!

So stop cursing your health efforts and start blessing them. You will soon be thinking, "Why didn't I do this sooner?" And your body will thank you for it!

Today's Prayer:

> God, from the beginning of the world You set in place seedtime and harvest time. I am planting seeds of good health right now. As time is passing until the harvest comes, help me to enjoy my life in the interim.
>
> Time does not stand still. I refuse to keep my life on hold until I reach my ideal size. I will do what I can at my current size, getting full enjoyment from my life now because tomorrow is not guaranteed to me.
>
> Help me to celebrate small victories, Lord. Help me to learn from my mistakes and pay special attention to what I am doing right so that I can repeat it.
>
> This is the day that You have made. I will rejoice and be glad in it. I will enjoy the body that I have today while enjoying the steps I am taking to change it for the better. Amen.

Focus Scripture:

- "This is the day the Lord has made; We will rejoice and be glad in it (Psalm 118:24)."

- "I know that nothing is better for them than to rejoice, and to do good in their lives, and also that every man should eat and drink and enjoy the good of all his labor—it is the gift of God (Ecclesiastes 3:12-13)."

Weight Loss Prayer Day 24: Redeem the Past

Recently in bible study, our pastor said something profound: "Most people act according to how they were raised, not how they were made."

His point was that many people, even Christians, act according to how their parents or other authority figures taught them. That is good if these people taught you according to Godly principles. But most of the time, that isn't the case. So you gain a worldly view of who you are and how you should act.

As an adult, you have a choice to make: "Do I want to keep living according to who the world says I am? Or do I want to live according to who God says I am?"

To live a life that pleases God, you must understand your identity in Him through Christ Jesus. As you understand your identity in Him, then you can start to understand God's ways and walk in them. To the world, you'll start looking like your Daddy!

Here are 3 confessions I recommend you speak based on scripture so that you can act according to your **real** image:

1. **"I am made in God's Image."** God blessed men and women to be a blessing to others. Evaluate your actions. Are you a blessing to your family? Your friends? Your employer or employees? If your actions are a curse rather than a blessing, then you are not acting according to how you were made. Ask God for help in these areas.

2. "I am fearfully and wonderfully made." I don't care how the world defines beauty; God created your features according to how He wanted you to look. You look **good**! Act like it – not in conceit, but in praise to God.

God loves variety; all you have to do is look around you to see that. He made people in different colors, shapes, sizes, heights, hair textures, etc. It's very sad that mankind has deemed some features as acceptable and some not.

But my advice to you? Stop disowning yourself because you don't fit man's standard! Own who you are! Take care of yourself and make healthy choices because you respect who God created you to be, not as a means to condemn yourself because you don't look like some man-made image.

3. "I am made the righteousness of God in Christ." This may be hard for you to believe, but it is true. As a believer in Jesus Christ, you are God's ambassador to those around you. You are to reflect His righteousness. According to Strong's concordance, righteousness means:

- Integrity
- Equity
- Justice
- Straightness
- Truth
- Sincerity

Now don't get it twisted; you have no righteousness of yourself. The righteousness in which you operate derives from believing in your heart and confessing with your mouth that Jesus is Lord. Whenever you act according to His Word in the bible and through the empowerment of the Holy Spirit, you are acting righteously.

I have to admit that I was nervous about this concept many years ago. You see, I wanted to fit in with my family, friends, and coworkers – not stand out as a Christian. But I had to make a decision: "Do I want to be a man-pleaser or do I want to be a God-pleaser?" I chose the latter because when I stand before God, I want Him to say to me, "Well done, thy good and faithful servant. Enter into the joy of your Lord!"

I recommend that you start evaluating your daily actions and determine if you are acting that way because it is how you were raised in the past (perhaps a worldly image) or if you are acting according to how you were made (God's image).

If you find yourself acting contrary to God's image, say to yourself, "That's not like me." If you can, then change your actions to match God's image at the earliest opportunity.

If you need help with that, then you can always go to God in prayer. I know He will be pleased to answer that request because it glorifies Him. But make the decision today because the world is looking for proof that God is alive and that He cares. You can be that proof!

Today's Prayer:

Lord, thank you that you redeem my past, guide my present, and secure my future! Help me to get past any painful experiences of the past and live according to how You made me.

You created me to reflect Your glory. So if there are any negative behaviors in my life that dull that reflection, then I want You to clean them up! I want others to see an accurate reflection of the difference you have made and are making in my life.

You created me in Your image. You created me fearfully and wonderfully. Help me to no longer neglect myself or insult myself because I don't fit a man-made standard. You love me exactly as I am. Help me to love myself enough to do what is best for myself, not just what is easy.

Empower me to reflect Your righteousness, God. Help me to make choices of integrity, justice, truth, and equity. I want to stay on the straight and narrow path, confident that You are keeping me in the center of Your will, which is a blessed place! Amen.

Focus Scriptures:

- "Then God said, Let Us make man in Our image, according to Our likeness...So God created man in His own image; in the image of God He created him; male and female He created them (Genesis 1:26-28)."

- "I will praise You, for I am fearfully and wonderfully made; Marvelous are Your works, And that my soul knows very well (Psalm 139:14)."

- "Now then, we are ambassadors for Christ, as though God were pleading through us: we implore you on Christ's behalf, be reconciled to God. For He made Him who knew no sin to be sin for us, that we might become the righteousness of God in Him (2 Corinthians 5:20-21)."

Weight Loss Prayer Day 25: Peace in my Choices

I've got a quick story for you: A young mother went to the grocery store with her young daughter. As they are strolling down the cookie aisle, the girl spots a bag of cookies she wants. The mother says 'No'. Instantly, the little girl falls out in a tantrum, crying and screaming for the cookies.

The mother sighs. Her daughter has just been diagnosed with diabetes. The mother knows that the cookies are not good for her daughter's condition. Yet, she wants to please her daughter and above all, wants her to be quiet because of embarrassment.

So the mother goes ahead and buys the cookies anyway. She gives her daughter a few in the car to pacify her on the way home.

Now, let's look at the same situation with a different mother and daughter. When the second girl falls out in the aisle crying and screaming for the cookies, the mother also remembers the girl's diabetic condition. She doesn't like saying 'No' to her daughter either and yet she says 'No' in spite of the discomfort because she realizes that she must protect her daughter from herself. She says 'No' out of love.

Which do you think was the better parent? I think you would agree that the second parent was better because she set boundaries for her child based on what was best for her long-term rather than what was just easy or felt good in the moment.

Consider that every day, you make dozens of choices that affect your health. In that role, you are like a parent. But you also have a child living inside of you (your flesh). Children are only concerned with getting what they want right now. They don't have the mental capacity to consider long-term consequences.

Mastering a spirit of self control requires deciding to become loving and responsible parent for yourself, like the second parent in the story. Your "child" is never going to change at the core level. Your child will always want to do what is quick, easy, and feels good in the moment.

Many people's health destinies are being written right now by poor daily choices because the child is in control.

One of my favorite scriptures is Proverbs 25:28:

> 'Whoever has no rule over his own spirit Is like a city broken down, without walls.'

When you lack self control in any area, you leave yourself open to all kinds of enemies, especially poor health.

So how can you turn things around if you have been a poor parent in terms of self control? Here are some principles to help you become a loving, responsible parent. The truth is that you already have the spirit of self control within since it is a fruit of the Spirit of life in Christ. You just have to learn how to use it.

1. Don't fight any unnecessary battles. A key principle of martial arts is "The best way to win a fight is to avoid getting into one in the first place." In the story, the mother could have avoided the daughter's drama by not even going down the cookie aisle!

Are you constantly exposing yourself to areas of weakness and hoping to come up with the willpower to resist them later? Big mistake. Set up boundaries in your environment to protect yourself from your weaknesses as much as possible.

2. Stay calm and balanced. Most of the time, we act in destructive ways when we are stressed or in emotional pain. Learn the art of calming yourself down through deep breathing. One breathing technique I practice when I am upset is the 4-2-8 breath. You breathe in for four counts, hold your breath for two counts, and breathe out for eight counts. Making your 'breathing out' longer than 'breathing in' automatically calms you down so you can think clearly.

It is also important that you keep your blood sugar stable throughout the day. Read labels and stay away from sugared drinks or any food that has more than 10 grams of sugar per serving. Also, be sure to eat several small, healthy meals each day. If you don't do these two things, you could be vulnerable to blood sugar crashes and you may not be able to think clearly enough to make wise decisions.

3. Always ask yourself, "What is best for me in the long run?" with every decision. This will give you a reality check so that you can know which is the best choice, not just what is the easy choice.

4. Act from wisdom, not from ease. Once you have determined what is best in the long run, watch your thoughts, mental pictures, and words. If these are not in line with that best decision, then change them so they become so. This can be challenging because your brain's default setting is probably in line with the child's desires right now rather than the loving parent.

So you need to switch to the loving parent setting, take your thoughts captive, and diligently line them up with your new decision.

Then, act on your better decision. The great news is that even though your child will still act like a child, she will soon learn that the parent is now in charge. If you are consistent, she will soon learn that tantrums don't get her anywhere and will stop fighting your attempts to change.

But again, don't waver. Be willing to live with the discomfort of saying 'no' to yourself. That feeling is only temporary, but once you begin to master the spirit of self control, you will gain peace and a greater sense of self-respect, which will make a positive impact in all other areas of your life.

Today's Prayer:

> Lord, I am so grateful that I am Your child! You said in Your Word that whoever humbles himself as a child is the greatest in the Kingdom of heaven. I humble myself before You Lord. I bow myself low enough so that you can work on me.
>
> I have been undisciplined in my actions in the past, so I need you to fill me with Your wisdom so that I can make wise decisions to take care of

myself. Help me to order my environment so that living a healthy lifestyle is easier. I want to avoid all unnecessary food fights!

I am thankful that whenever I feel stressed or overwhelmed, I can run to You for comfort rather than the enemy's destructive strongholds. Your mercies are new every morning. Have mercy on me, Lord. I need You every hour to help me make wise choices. I know You are faithful to be with me because Your Word says You will! You are the ultimate loving Parent and I follow your example.

Focus Scriptures:

- 'Whoever has no rule over his own spirit Is like a city broken down, without walls (Proverbs 25:28).'

- "Therefore whoever humbles himself as this little child is the greatest in the kingdom of heaven (Matthew 18:4)."

- "But I will sing of Your power; Yes, I will sing aloud of Your mercy in the morning; For You have been my defense And refuge in the day of my trouble (Psalm 59:16)."

- "Trust in the Lord with all your heart, And lean not on your own understanding; In all your ways acknowledge Him, And He shall direct your paths (Proverbs 3:5-6)."

Weight Loss Prayer Day 26: Walk in the Spirit

In John 14:16-18, Jesus makes a promise: "And I will pray the Father, and He will give you another Helper, that He may abide with you forever— the Spirit of truth, whom the world cannot receive, because it neither sees Him nor knows Him; but you know Him, for He dwells with you and will be in you. I will not leave you orphans; I will come to you."

The Holy Spirit is not an angel; He is the dynamic, muscle power of God. He is God. Remember, we worship a truine God, one God three persons - Father, Son, and the Holy Spirit.

In John 16:13-15, Jesus tells you the Holy Spirit's role in your life. The Holy Spirit:

*   Guides you into all truth
*   Speaks to you what He hears from the Lord
*   Tells you things to come
*   Takes of Jesus and declares it to you

So the power of God lives in you and dwells with you! Now you might wonder, if I have the power of God living inside of me, then how come I deal with all of these negative emotions? How come I feel like a candy bar has power over me?

Well, it is true when you become a disciple of Christ, you now have the power of the living God inside of you. But still have your old mind and it must be renewed to the thoughts of God through His word - the Bible.

When you do that, you'll be able to hear the Holy Spirit's voice and obey His leading. Now how do you know if the voice that you are hearing is really the voice of the Holy Spirit? For me, I think of four guidelines:

1. The voice of the Holy Spirit is still and small. He doesn't scream at you, but His voice is quiet and reasonable.

2. The voice of the Holy Spirit always agrees with the Word of God. Again, that is why it is so important that you study the word for yourself so that you can determine if the voice you're hearing agrees with the word you are studying.

3. Does the choice have the potential to bear Spiritual fruit? In Galatians 5:22-23, we are told what the Spiritual fruit is: "But the fruit of the Spirit is love, joy, peace, longsuffering, kindness, goodness, faithfulness, gentleness, self-control. Against such there is no law."

4. Finally, the last guideline is a companion to the notion of Spiritual fruit; Does the choice bring you peace? Now notice that I did not say if the choice is easy! In all likelihood, it won't be easy simply because Spiritual choices war against fleshly choices. But the good news is not only does the Holy Spirit help you make the right choices, but He gives you the power to walk them out. And He has the power to comfort you as you make those hard choices if you ask Him.

When you make Godly choices, you have an opportunity to get to know God better and even to get to know yourself better.

Jesus said that the kingdom of God is within and Romans 14:17 defines what the kingdom of God is: "for the kingdom of God is not eating and drinking, but righteousness, peace, and joy in the Holy Spirit."

That is the way that God's people are meant to live. It doesn't mean that you will never face trouble, but it does mean that you will emerge victorious.

As you affirm God's love continually, acknowledge the Holy Spirit, listen to His voice and obey it, you will bear fruit that glorifies God. In John 15:8, Jesus says, "by this my father is glorified, that you bear much fruit. So you will be my disciples."

Today is your new beginning. I recommend that you use the Scriptures mentioned in this book to begin your own Bible study so that you truly can know that God loves you. He wants you to live the abundant life that Jesus died to give you and to bring Him pleasure in the process!

Today's Prayer:

> Lord, Jesus constantly exhorted those who listened to Him, "Them who have ears, let him hear!" Oh may I have ears to hear when the Holy Spirit speaks to me and a heart to obey.

I know the Holy Spirit lives within me and empowers me to do everything that You are calling me to do. I will be diligent to read and apply your Word so I can discern truth from error. I set my mind daily on the things of the Spirit.

The more Spiritually minded I am, the more life I experience and have to share with others. I want others to taste and see that You are good. That can only happen with the Spiritual fruit that I share with them.

Jesus said that the kingdom of God is within. I want to live in Your kingdom, Lord. I want righteousness, peace, and joy to reign in my daily life. As I obey Your Holy Spirit, Your will is done on Earth as it is in heaven. Praise You Lord; Let Your kingdom come! Amen.

Focus Scriptures:

- "For I consider that the sufferings of this present time are not worthy to be compared with the glory which shall be revealed in us. For the earnest expectation of the creation eagerly waits for the revealing of the sons of God (Romans 8:18-20)."

- "But the fruit of the Spirit is love, joy, peace, longsuffering, kindness, goodness, faithfulness, gentleness, self-control. Against such there is no law (Galatians 5:22-23)."

- "for the kingdom of God is not eating and drinking, but righteousness, peace, and joy in the Holy Spirit (Romans 14:17)."

- "For to be carnally minded is death, but to be Spiritually-minded is life and peace (Romans 8:6)."

Weight Loss Prayer Day 27: Credit Small Victories

How many times have you gotten frustrated with yourself because you knew you should do the right thing, but couldn't make yourself do it? It's a common story for those who strive to practice better health habits. However, I've got three guidelines that can help you change for the better.

Let's say that you have issues with emotional eating. You know that it's not a healthy behavior to practice but you find yourself doing it anyway. You beat yourself up every time you do it.

When you condemn yourself for weaknesses, all you do is set yourself for more stress, frustration and depression. Which makes it likely that you will fall back on your weaknesses even more!

But what if you take a different approach?

Try this: The next time you finding yourself acting in a way you don't want to, extend some grace to yourself. The second you recognize your error say to yourself immediately: "See, that's why I need a Savior."

Call it getting some WINS: "Why I Need a Savior"

None of us are perfect, but when you are humble in admitting you need the grace of a Savior to help you in your time of need, you use your imperfections as an opportunity to draw closer to God. You invite God into your situation rather than insisting that you can do it alone and don't need any help.

Now, WINS aren't an excuse to keep making the same mistakes. Once you admit the WIN, just simply say to God: "Help me in this area. Show me how to replace my weakness with your strength." And then apply the wisdom He gives you.

The second guideline is strive for progress, not perfection. Every time you are faced with the choice to practice a negative habit, make it a game to exert just a little more self control than you did the last time.

For example, you always eat a candy bar or chips as an afternoon snack. Rather than stopping it altogether (although that's terrific if you can do that), then drink a glass of water first and cut the snack amount in half. That is progress, so you win! You are still going to the same destination, a healthier you, but you are just choosing to take a slower route to get there.

Another progress step could be making preparations for your afternoon hunger. You take a high fiber fruit such as an apple, pear, or orange with you so that you turn to it instead of the vending machine.

Again, think progress not perfection. As you make those "progress" efforts with small choices, your confidence will grow and you will be ready to make bigger, better choices.

Finally, get some accountability. It is very easy to practice bad habits in secret. But when you commit to changing for the better and get a trusted friend or coach who can help you keep your promise to yourself, you bring what is done in secret to light so that it can be handled.

Keep this critical principle in mind: If you don't handle bad habits, eventually those bad habits will handle you!

Ask yourself right now: Are you handling your habits or are they handling you?

If the answer is the second one, you can turn things around today by getting some WINS under your belt. Then get ready because your life will change! Guaranteed.

Today's Prayer:

> Lord, I need the Savior's grace to help me in my time of need. I am confronted every day with my weaknesses and imperfections. I need Your strength to carry me through every challenge.
>
> Help me not to despise my small beginnings; rather let me celebrate every sign of progress. I am not living a diet; I am living my life and I am determined to enjoy every day of my life no matter what size I am.
>
> I love You, Lord! I love the person You created me to be. Thank You for this opportunity to get to discover Your faithfulness in a very personal way! Amen.

Focus Scriptures:

- "And this is eternal life, that they may know You, the only true God, and Jesus Christ whom You have sent (John 17:3)."

- "He who is faithful in what is least is faithful also in much; and he who is unjust in what is least is unjust also in much (Luke 16:10)."

Weight Loss Prayer Day 28: Reasonable Expectations

I don't know anyone who, when attempting to lose weight and get healthy, doesn't want to get results as fast as possible. Remember though, your ultimate goal is to build a healthy lifestyle that you can live in. That will likely require that you try different methods until you find the one that fits the way you live. This is normal part of the change process.

While I can't promise that you will lose 30 pounds in 30 days with this approach, you can get more lasting results if you use wisdom in creating your weight loss plan and through setting reasonable expectations.

Keep the following principle in mind: You will only get out of your efforts what you are willing to put in. This is a Biblical principle: "Do not be deceived, God is not mocked; for whatever a man sows, this he will also reap" (Galatians 6:7).

So to reap excellent health, you must sow the habits that lead to the harvest.

To create unstoppable motivation while you are waiting for your results to manifest, you also need to go deeper than the shallow reasons for wanting to shed pounds. Looking good or fitting into a certain size is an okay goal but that is not enough to keep you going when you want to quit. God did not put you here just for your own pleasure – He created you to make a difference.

Consider the many ways that getting fit will positively impact your life and the lives of others:

- It will give you energy to fulfill your God-given purpose
- It will empower you to be a better spouse, parent, employee, or business owner
- It will enable you to be a positive role model and perhaps influence others to take care of themselves
- It will strengthen you mentally and emotionally so you can handle life's challenges well
- It will give you the discipline you need to reach your goals in all areas of your life

Our bodies are the temples, the house of the Lord. Taking care of them is part of our reasonable service and that responsibility does not end until we leave our bodies behind to go on to our heavenly homes. So commit to this good work – and see it through to the end.

Today's Prayer:

> Lord, I need Your wisdom to help me to set reasonable expectations on my weight loss journey. The world tries to entice me to go after quick fixes. But I've been down that road and I don't want to lose weight quickly only to gain it back! I want to end weight as an issue in my life forever. I want to build a healthy lifestyle for lasting results.

I want all of the blessings of good health: energy to fulfill the purpose to which You have called me, empowerment to be a positive role model, mental and emotional strength to handle life's challenges well, and discipline to reach my goals in all areas of my life.

You said in Your word that You want me to prosper and be in health as my soul prospers. I know I will achieve it in due season with Your help. Amen.

Focus Scriptures:

- "Do not be deceived, God is not mocked; for whatever a man sows, this he will also reap (Galatians 6:7)"

- "And let us not grow weary while doing good, for in due season we shall reap if we do not lose heart (Galatians 6:9)."

- "Beloved, I pray that you may prosper in all things and be in health, just as your soul prospers (3 John 1:2)."

Weight Loss Prayer Day 29: Be Grateful

When I was six years old, I jumped off the roof of our house.

It was one of the memories that came back to me as I was meditating on the ways God has protected me over the years. Thanks to him, my naive attempt to fly only gave me strained back, not broken bones.

The reason I thought about that incident is because of a book I read called "How to Listen to God" by Dr. Charles Stanley. I bought this book several years ago but had never read it completely. Isn't it funny how you can sometimes avoid the knowledge that you need the most?

I know it was fear that was keeping me from reading that book. Deep down, I knew that once I read it, I could no longer do "business as usual." I would be accountable to use what I'd learned.

There's a saying that if you do what you've always done, you'll always get what you've always got. Well, I wanted something different so I was ready to do something different. I picked up the book.

In one part of the book, Dr. Stanley discusses the process of Christian meditation. As an example, he used King David and how approached his meditation time before the Lord:

1. He meditated on what God had done for him in the past.

2. He meditated on God's character – His greatness, His grace, and His goodness.

3. He meditated on God's promises.

4. He made his request to God – and sat still waiting for God's counsel.

I used this process and how powerful it is! I remembered incidents from my past that I hadn't thought about in years. I know I only got through because of the grace of God. I also can clearly see times when he protected me from danger and bad decisions.

As I meditated using the first three steps, I was smiling and felt deep gratitude for God's faithfulness.

By the time I made my request about a business dilemma I had, His voice came through very clearly with the answer. When I got up from my prayer, I felt a fullness in my heart I had never experienced. I felt a renewed sense of confidence and optimism about the future.

Do you need a new beginning, a miracle, or a breakthrough in your life? Then take the previous wisdom and apply it to your life. You'll be grateful you did.

God loves you and He has your answer. It's time that you breakthrough to a victorious life!

Today's Prayer:

Lord, thank You for all that You've done for me! You never leave me nor forsake me and you love me without limits. I praise Your great and awesome name. I praise You for your lovingkindness and Your tender mercies. I am grateful that You have called me out of darkness into Your marvelous light.

I am grateful to be walking on this journey with You. Through Your son Jesus Christ, I am more than a conqueror! I have already won this weight loss battle and I am merely waiting for the manifestation of it in the physical realm.

I treasure Your wisdom Lord; I treasure the fact that You lead me and guide me in the way that I should go. I am thankful that in You there is nothing missing and nothing broken. I am truly blessed! Help me Lord to stay focused on the big picture rather than being preoccupied with petty grievances. Help me to realize that no matter how bad things are on some days, there is always a reason to celebrate because I am Your child. Amen.

Focus Scriptures:

- "Why are you cast down, O my soul? And why are you disquieted within me? I hope in God; For I shall yet praise Him, The help of my countenance and my God (Psalm 42:11)."

- "Enter into His gates with thanksgiving, And into His courts with praise. Be thankful to Him, and bless His name (Psalm 100:4)."

- "And let the peace of God rule in your hearts, to which also you were called in one body; and be thankful (Colossians 3:15)."

Weight Loss Prayer Day 30: Maintain my Success

Whenever you want to do something great in your life, your faith that you will succeed will be **tested**.

This is especially true when you are working to change your weight and health.

- Your resolve will be tested
- Your desire will be tested
- Your patience will be tested

Yet, you can pass every faith test when you know how to defeat faith's biggest enemy.

What enemy am I talking about?

Forgetfulness. Remember this phrase: "Forgetfulness is the enemy of faith."

Think about it. How many times have you started a health improvement plan with great enthusiasm – only to abandon it a few weeks later?

Did you ever wonder why this happens?

Many times, it happens because we conveniently forget about the reason we wanted to make the change – or else decide (subconsciously) that the process to change isn't worth the effort!

If you are believing God to help you change your health for the better, then you must combat forgetfulness in three areas:

- Forgetting about God's mighty Power
- Forgetting about your Purpose in better health
- Forgetting about the Plan necessary to achieve your purpose

Let's deal with each one:

- **Forgetting about God's Power:** Remember – there is **nothing** too hard for God!

Most of us have read the story of the 12 men sent out to spy the Promised Land (see Numbers, chapter 13). In the story, God promised the Israelites a land of "milk and honey." And yet when it was time to take over the land, they refused to do it because of the obstacles they would face.

They forgot that this same God delivered them out of slavery in Egypt. He defeated their enemy and parted the Red Sea so they could cross safely.

To remember God's power in your life, start a "Journal of Testimony" to document all the blessings God has done for you in the past and as you live in the present, write down every blessing as it happens – before you forget.

Then when your resolve faith is tested, you can open your "JOT" book and be encouraged that if God helped you before, He will do it again.

- **Forgetting about your Purpose in better health:**

Answer this question – why do you want to lose weight and get healthy?

If you don't bother to write down your purpose in achieving better health and review it often, then forgetfulness has just defeated your faith.

Make your reasons powerful and meaningful for you. You need to see the end of the journey and make your vision so magnetic that you can't help but be drawn to it. Remind yourself of your vision as often as possible so your faith remains strong.

- **Forgetting about the Plan necessary to achieve your purpose**

I used to **hate** counting anything regarding my eating. I didn't care if it was counting calories, carbs, fiber, points, whatever. I did not like to count. So thankfully, in my first 8 years on this health journey, I didn't have to. I reached my ideal size and stay there for several years. As long as I maintained a healthy eating pattern 90% of the time and allowed myself treats in moderation 10% of the time, I was good.

But then something changed.

I found myself gaining weight. My clothes started getting tight and energy level headed south. My diet hadn't changed much, so what was going on? Then the lightbulb came on – I am getting older. My hormonal balance has changed. I needed make adjustments in my portion sizes. I can't eat as much as I used to.

As much as I didn't want to admit it, I needed to take the step of counting for a season.

I use a phone app and website to do this. There have been times when I conveniently want to "forget" to record something I've eaten, but I remind myself: "Forgetfulness is the enemy of faith." So I record because I want to remember to do the things that will help me stay on track.

My pastor often says "A sharp pencil is better than a good memory."

The reward for my faith is that I am within shouting distance of my regular size. It feels great!

What plan do you need to practice to reach your vision? Whether you use an app or a website or journal or a piece of paper, you need a method to help keep you accountable for remembering to do it.

Don't let the enemy of forgetfulness rob you of your future vision. Power, Purpose, Plan. Remember, remember, remember!

Today's Prayer:

Lord, now that I'm reaching the end of my weight loss journey and celebrating how far I've come, never let me forget where I came from. It's tempting to want to forget the challenges and pain of the past. And yet, I know that they helped to shape who I am today.

I've seen your mighty power at work all along this journey. You've revealed to me the purpose of maintaining good health and through Your wisdom, I developed the plan to succeed. I need Your help to maintain what I've gained.

Help me to recognize any deceptions that the enemy tries to feed to me to try to convince me to go back to my old ways. I've seen where those ways lead and I don't want to go back! So help me not be complacent, but continue to be sober and vigilant.

I celebrate the victory in You, Lord. When people ask me about my weight loss, I will be careful not to take the credit that belongs to You. Without You, I am nothing but in You, I have everything! Amen.

Focus Scriptures:

- "You shall remember that you were a slave in the land of Egypt, and the Lord your God redeemed you; therefore I command you this thing today (Deuteronomy 15:15)."

"Oh, give thanks to the Lord!
Call upon His name;
Make known His deeds among the peoples!
Sing to Him, sing psalms to Him;
Talk of all His wondrous works!
Glory in His holy name;
Let the hearts of those rejoice who seek the Lord!
Seek the Lord and His strength;
Seek His face evermore!
Remember His marvelous works which He has done,
His wonders, and the judgments of His mouth,
O seed of Israel His servant,
You children of Jacob, His chosen ones (1 Chronicles 16:8-13)!"

About the Author

"Just wanted to again thank you for sharing your unique and engaging presentation to help us take back our temples! You were truly a blessing and I know that many were enlightened by what you shared."

- Danese Turner, Turner Chapel AME, Marietta GA

Kimberly Taylor is the creator of **Takebackyourtemple.com**, a website that inspires Christians to Spiritual, emotional, and physical health. She is the author of the ebook *Take Back Your Temple* and the books ***The Weight Loss scriptures***, ***God's Word is Food***, and **many others**.

Once 240 pounds and a size 22, Kim lost 85 pounds through renewing her mind and taking action upon God's word. Her experience led her to establish the Take Back Your Temple website. "Take Back Your Temple" is a prayer that asks God to take control of your body and your life so He can use them for His purpose and agenda.

Kim's weight loss success story has been featured on CBN's *The 700 Club,* and in *Prevention Magazine*, *Essence Magazine*, *Charisma Magazine* and many other magazines and newspapers. She has also been interviewed on various radio programs.

Kim exhorts people of faith to become good stewards of all the resources God has given to them, including time, money, talents, and physical health. "I am passionate about empowering others to adopt healthy lifestyles so they can fulfill their God-given purpose," she says.

"My dream is for God's people to stand apart because we are healthy, prosperous and living the abundant life to which we are called. I want non-believers to look at us and want what we have: Spiritual, mental, and physical wholeness. Then when they ask us what we are doing differently, we can tell them about Jesus, the author and finisher of our faith."

Stay Connected

You can stay connected with Kimberly Taylor through the following channels:

Amazon Author Page

You can learn about all of Kimberly Taylor's books and eBooks available on Amazon.com at one convenient location:
https://www.amazon.com/author/kimberlyytaylor

Take Back Your Temple website

Kimberly's website, **www.takebackyourtemple.com/** shares her testimony of deliverance from emotional overeating through the change God made in her heart and mind. Hundreds of free articles on the website encourage other Christians on the road to Spiritual, emotional, and physical health.

Facebook

You can connect with Kimberly on Facebook at **http://www.facebook.com/takebackyourtemple**. She also moderates a secret Facebook support group comprised of believers who struggle with emotional eating and are working to change their health. Details on how to join the group are available at *takebackyourtemple.com*.

Twitter

Follow Kimberly on Twitter at
twitter.com/tbytkimberly

Pinterest
You can view Kim's Pinterest boards at
http://pinterest.com/tbyt/

All paperback versions of this series were published
through **StartYourBook.org**.